FALL IN LOVE STAY IN LOVE

Other books by Willard F. Harley, Jr.

His Needs, Her Needs
Love Busters
5 Steps to Romantic Love
Your Love and Marriage
The Four Gifts of Love
Surviving an Affair
Give and Take
Marriage Insurance

FALL IN LOVE STAY IN LOVE

WILLARD F. HARLEY, JR.

Fleming H. Revell

A Division of Baker Book House Co
Grand Rapids, Michigan 49516

© 2001 by Willard F. Harley, Jr.

Published by Fleming H. Revell
a division of Baker Book House Company
P.O. Box 6287, Grand Rapids, MI 49516-6287

Printed in the United States of America

Library of Congress Cataloging-in-Publication Data

Harley, Willard F.
    Fall in love, stay in love / Willard F. Harley, Jr.
        p.   cm.
    ISBN 0-8007-1793-7
    1. Marriage. 2. Love. I. Title

HQ734 .H283   2001
306.81—dc21   2001031831

For current information about all releases from Baker Book House, visit our web site:
http://www.bakerbooks.com

CONTENTS

part one

SETTING THE STAGE

chapter one

HOW I LEARNED TO SAVE
MARRIAGES

I've been counseling couples with marital problems for over forty years, and during that time I've learned what makes marriages succeed and what makes them fail. But I sure didn't start out knowing that. In fact my first ten years of marriage counseling taught me only one thing—that I was not qualified to counsel. Although almost every couple I saw was sincerely grateful for my advice, I cannot think of a single couple I actually helped. Most of their marriages ended in divorce, and the rest continued to have serious problems.

Miserable Beginnings

One couple I counseled was my pastor and his wife. The choir director and my pastor's wife were having an affair, and I tried to help end it. I explained to her how the affair was threatening the happiness and success of their children and ruining her husband's ministry, and how the choir director's wife and children needed him just as much as her husband and children needed her. But she replied that since God was a God of love, he had approved her relationship with the choir director by giving her the feeling of love for him.

I had come face-to-face with the irrationality that the feeling of love can create, and I didn't know how to handle it. Eventually my pastor's wife and the choir director divorced their respective spouses and married each other. The children in both families suffered greatly throughout the entire ordeal, and to the best of my knowledge are still suffering. The church began a downward spiral from which it never recovered and it eventually disbanded. This tragedy took place because my pastor's wife had fallen out of love with her husband and fallen in love with the choir director. (Incidentally, after a few years of an unhappy marriage, the choir director had another affair and divorced my pastor's former wife.)

My pastor was not alone in the tragedy of divorce. His was just one of a host of marriages caught up in a wave that was overwhelming families in the mid-1960s. This trend toward divorce would escalate over the next twenty years until more than half of all marriages were ending in divorce. I didn't know that at the time. I thought that this failure was, at least in part, due to my inexperience. I blamed myself, thinking that I should not have tried to give advice, that I should have left it to an "expert."

This trend toward divorce would escalate over the next twenty years until more than half of all marriages were ending in divorce.

"Expert" Failures

Over the next few years, couples kept asking for my advice regarding marriage, especially after I earned a Ph.D. degree in psychology. So instead of turning these people away, I decided to learn enough about marriage counseling to help save their marriages—I decided to become an expert. After all, if scientists could send men to the moon, surely they would know how to save marriages.

I read books on marital therapy, was supervised by experts in the field, and worked in a clinic that specialized in marital therapy and claimed to be the best in Minnesota. But none of it helped. I was still unable to save marriages. Almost everyone who came to me for help ended up like my pastor—divorced.

But in my effort to become an expert, I made a crucial discovery: I wasn't the only one failing to help couples. Almost everyone else working with me in the clinic was failing as well! My supervisor was failing, the director of the clinic was failing, and so were the other marriage counselors who worked with me. And then I made the most astonishing discovery of all: Most of the marital experts in America were also failing.

What made me unique among marriage counselors was my curiosity to know if my efforts really worked. Hardly any other therapist I knew wanted to know about the outcome of his or her therapy. Many did not know they were failing because they never followed up on their cases to see how the marriages were doing. But I had access to their cases, so I did the follow-up for them. In the clinic where I worked, I couldn't find any therapists who were actually saving marriages. And to make matters worse, many of these marital experts were divorced themselves. The director of the clinic, and creator of their "successful" marital therapy program, was divorced shortly after I left the clinic.

Was I working with a particularly inept group of therapists? Or were the problems I witnessed only the tip of the iceberg? To satisfy my curiosity, I did what I should have done in the very beginning of my venture—I read studies that evaluated the effectiveness of marital therapy in general. To my surprise, I learned that marital therapy throughout America had the lowest success rate of any form of therapy. In one study, I read that less than 25 percent of those surveyed felt that marriage counseling did them any good whatsoever, and a higher percentage felt that it did them more harm than good.

Searching for Answers

What a challenge! Marriages were breaking up at an unprecedented rate, and no one knew how to fix them! So I made it my own personal ambition to find the answer, and I looked for that answer not in books, scholarly articles, or experts but rather among those who came to me for answers—couples who were about to divorce. I stopped counseling and started listening as spouses told me why they were ready to throw in the towel. What did they have when they decided to marry that they lost somewhere along the way, and what would it take for them to find it again?

By 1975 I had discovered why I and so many other marital therapists were having trouble saving marriages—we did not understand what makes marriages work. We were all so preoccupied with what seemed to make them fail that we overlooked what made them succeed. Couples would come to my office for counseling because they were making each other miserable. So I thought, as most others thought, if I could simply get them to communicate more clearly, resolve their conflicts more effectively, and stop fighting with each other so much, their marriage would be saved. But that wasn't the answer.

Couple after couple explained to me that they didn't marry each other because they were communicating so clearly or resolving their conflicts effectively or were not fighting with each other. They married because they found each other irresistible—they were in love. But by the time they came to my office, they had lost that feeling of love. Many actually found each other repulsive. And one of the most important reasons that they were communicating so poorly, resolving their conflicts so ineffectively, and fighting so much was that they had lost their feeling of love.

They married because they found each other irresistible—they were in love.

If your marriage was in trouble and I asked you what would it take for you and your spouse to be happily married again, what would you say? My guess is that at first you might not imagine that ever happening. You might think that the only way you could be happily married would be if you were married to someone else! But if I persisted, and you were able to reflect on my question, you might say what others have told me: "We would be happily married again if we were in love."

Over and over that's what couples told me when I asked that question. But what they didn't tell me was also instructive. They didn't tell me that if they communicated better or resolved their conflicts or stopped fighting so much, they would be happily married. Granted, poor communication, failure to resolve conflicts, and fighting all *contribute* to the loss of love. But these are also *symptoms* of lost love. In other words, I began to realize that if I wanted to save marriages, I would have to go beyond improving communication. I would have to learn how to restore love.

With this insight, I began to attack emotional issues with couples rather than rational issues. My primary goal in marital therapy changed from resolving conflicts to restoring love. If I knew how to restore love, I reasoned, then conflict resolution might not be as much of an issue.

My background as a psychologist has taught me that learned associations trigger most of our emotional reactions. Whenever something is presented repeatedly with a physically induced emotion, it tends to trigger that emotion all by itself. For example, if you flash the color blue along with an electric shock, and the color red with a soothing back rub, eventually the color blue will tend to upset you and the color red will tend to relax you.

Applying the same principle to the feeling of love, I theorized that love might be nothing more than a learned association. If someone were to be present often enough when I was feeling particularly good, the person's presence in general might be enough to trigger that good feeling—something we have come to know as the feeling of love.

Success at Last

I could not have been more correct in my analysis. I found that this hypothesis proved to be true—and it's the key to being a successful marriage counselor. I began to encourage couples to try to do whatever it took to make each other happy and avoid doing what made each other unhappy. For the very first couple I counseled with my new approach, the feeling of love was restored and their marriage was saved.

So from that point on, each time I saw a couple, I simply asked each of them what the other could do that would make them the happiest, and whatever it was, that was their first assignment. Of course, not every couple really knew what would make them happy, and not every spouse was willing to do it. So I wasn't successful with every couple I counseled, but I was on the right track.

As I perfected my approach to marriage counseling, I began to understand what it is that husbands and wives need from each other to trigger the feeling of love. So I helped couples identify those needs. I also became increasingly effective at motivating them to meet whatever needs were identified, even when they didn't feel like doing it at first. Before long, I was helping almost every couple fall in love, and thereby avoid divorce.

Up to this point in my career, I was teaching psychology full-time and counseling part-time. I did not charge couples for my services because I knew I had been ineffective in saving marriages. But as soon as my new method proved to be successful, I quit my secure job as a professor and took the risky step of earning my living as a marriage counselor. After one month it was clear that I had made the right choice—my schedule was full and I was saving marriages.

> I began to encourage couples to try to do whatever it took to make each other happy and avoid doing what made each other unhappy.

The reason my pastor's wife was willing to sacrifice everything that was important to her—her marriage, her children, her career, even her faith—was that she was in love with the choir director. If I had been able to redirect her feeling of love from the choir director to her husband, their marriage would have been saved and the tragic events that followed would have been avoided. It was her feeling of love that got her into the mess she was in, but the feeling of love would also have saved her. I only wish I knew then what I know now.

And I want you to know what I know now. I want you to fully understand how important your feeling of love, and your spouse's feeling of love, is to the survival of your marriage. Whether you know it or not, or whether you believe it or not, your marriage depends on the love you and your spouse have for each other. But I want you to do more than understand the importance of love in marriage. I want you to be able to re-create it, if it's been lost, and sustain it, if you are still in love. By the time you finish reading this book, you will have the tools to do just that. I've written this book to help you turn a potential disaster into a personal triumph!

Since the feeling of love is so important in marriage, I will begin by helping you understand what the feeling of love is. I'll do this by introducing you to the first basic concept I created to help couples understand the rise and fall of their love for each other. I call it the Love Bank.

Key Principles

- The feeling of love is such a powerful emotion that to sustain it people are willing to sacrifice almost anything—their marriage, their children's happiness, their career, and even their faith.

- When spouses are in love with each other, there is no risk of divorce because they want to be with each other at all costs. But when they are not in love, they lose their most important emotional reason to be together, and the risk of divorce is very high, even if they have learned to communicate effectively with each other.

- Marriage counselors who focus attention on communication skills and conflict resolution cannot save marriages if their efforts do not lead to triggering the feeling of love in couples they counsel.

- To save their marriage, a couple must learn how to fall in love and stay in love with each other.

chapter two

THE LOVE
BANK

Let me ask you a very personal question. Why did you decide to marry your spouse? Did you discuss the pros and cons with friends and relatives? Did you take a test to determine if you were compatible? Did you find that your spouse met criteria that predicted your marital success?

Maybe you did some of these things, but I doubt that they had much effect on your decision to marry. Most couples marry each other because they are in love. And when you're in love, you cannot imagine living without each other. You probably married your spouse because you found him or her irresistible.

That's how it was for my wife, Joyce, and me. Long before I asked her to marry me, we both knew that we were unhappy when we were not seeing each other regularly. We broke up a few times so that we could date others, but whenever that happened, we missed each other terribly. We were in love.

We eventually came to the conclusion that life without each other would be a tragic mistake, and so to avoid disaster we married much sooner than we had originally planned. Joyce was only nineteen; I was twenty-one. Thirty-eight years later, with two married children and four grandchildren, we still cannot imagine what life would be like without each other. And we still find each other irresistible.

Joyce and I do not have a good marriage because we were meant for each other. It may seem that way, but it isn't true. The reason we are still in love with each other is that we have deliberately done what it takes to stay in love. We are living proof that a married couple can be in love throughout their lifetime as long as they follow the "rules."

But before I explain these rules that will help you fall in love and stay in love, you need to understand how love works. What is it that made you fall in love with each other? What may have caused you to lose that love? And if it is lost, how can your love be restored?

What Is Love?

There are two kinds of love in marriage. The first kind of love is what Joyce and I had for each other before marriage and still have today. I call it **romantic love.** It is the feeling of being in love—finding someone irresistible.

> **Romantic Love**
>
> The feeling of being in love—finding someone irresistible.

Romantic love is not something mystical or magical. In fact it is an emotion that your brain creates whenever certain conditions are met. And your brain can eliminate the emotion when other conditions are met. It can be turned on and off with predictable certainty, and it can even be measured scientifically.

After I discovered that helping couples fall in love saved their marriages, I wanted to be sure my methods were actually creating the feeling of love in the couples I counseled. So I designed a test to measure whether or not they were in love with each other.

I started out with about one hundred questions that I thought would measure the feeling of love, and I gave those questions to several hundred people who told me they were in love and several hundred people who told me they were not in love. A statistical item analysis picked twenty questions out of the original one hundred that were the most highly correlated to being in love.

18

I called my final test the Love Bank Inventory. Each item was to be answered with a number from −3 (definitely no) to +3 (definitely yes). A zero meant that you didn't really know how you felt.

I won't give you the entire test, or even let you know how it's scored, because when couples are not in love, they are usually so offended by each other's low scores that they feel like giving up. But I'll show you a few sample questions, so you'll have a better understanding of how I measured the feeling of love.

These questions get at the very essence of what the feeling of romantic love really is. It's a feeling of incredible attraction for someone of the opposite sex. For those who have it, it's a feeling that is unmistakable and it can be sustained indefinitely.

If my goal as a marital therapist is to help couples re-create their feeling of love for each other, you can see how important it is for me to be able to measure that love. Otherwise, how do I know if my methods are succeeding or failing? So each time a couple sees me for a counseling session, they must complete the Love Bank Inventory. That way I know how close they are to experiencing the first kind of love.

There is a second kind of love in marriage that is also very important. I call it **caring love** because it represents a decision to care for your spouse—to do what you can to make your spouse happy.

People can have caring love in many types of relationships. The love for your children, for example, is caring love, as is the love you have for your pets. In fact we often care for people we don't even know when we decide to invest time and resources in charitable organizations that help people. As a psychologist, I spend much of my time caring for strangers.

Sample Questions

Do you usually have a good feeling whenever you think about _____?

Would you rather be with _____ than anyone else?

Do you enjoy telling _____ your deepest feelings and most private experiences?

Do you feel a "chemistry" between you and _____?

Does _____ bring out the best in you?

Although I have not done it, I could have easily developed a test to measure your willingness to care for your spouse. It would include questions about how concerned you are about your spouse's happiness, and what you have done to try to improve your spouse's quality of life. But a test of care would not necessarily predict your marital happiness and success. That's because your care may not actually trigger your spouse's feeling of romantic love toward you. For example, you may want your spouse to be happy more than anything else. And you may be willing to do whatever it takes to make your spouse happy. But if you don't know what to do or how to do it, your good intentions will not get the job done.

> **Caring Love**
>
> A decision to try to do what you can to make someone happy—a willingness and effort to care for someone.

If your spouse enjoys hamburgers and hates hot dogs, and you don't know it, the hot dog casserole you made with all your love will cause you to be associated with his or her gagging and choking. Your hard work will go for naught, and it would be better if you had done nothing. But if you put your energy into a hamburger platter, you will hit the bull's eye. Those hamburgers might be just enough to trigger the feeling of love.

Some marriage counselors think that all your spouse really wants is to know that you care. But they're wrong. Knowing you care is not enough to create romantic love. I've counseled hundreds of couples that care about each other yet have filed for divorce. But I have yet to know of a couple in love with each other who are even contemplating divorce.

The reason that caring love is not enough to save a marriage is that good intentions carry you only so far. Only when your intent inspires acts of care *that actually cause your spouse to be happy* can it save your marriage. And that brings up an important relationship between romantic love and caring love. When your acts of care meet your spouse's important emotional needs, they trigger romantic love. In other words, your spouse's romantic love for you is a good litmus test of the effectiveness of your care for your spouse. If your care makes your spouse happy, he or she will be in love with you. If your spouse is no longer in love with you, you may care for your spouse, but your acts of care are ineffective in making him or her happy.

It goes without saying that without caring love, it's very difficult to maintain romantic love. Unless you and your spouse care for each other—are willing to do what it takes to make each other happy—it's not likely that you will trigger the feeling of love. But while caring love is a necessary ingredient to a successful marriage, it is not the most important ingredient. In the end, it's romantic love that keeps your marriage secure.

How Is Romantic Love Created and Destroyed?

Most people regard the feeling of love as one of life's great and wonderful mysteries. It's certainly great and wonderful, but as I have already mentioned, it's not a mystery. I have found the feeling of love to be quite predictable. And it's that predictability that makes my job possible. By understanding the factors that create and destroy the feeling of love, I show married couples how to rediscover love for each other after it's been lost.

To help my clients understand the predictability of love, I invented the concept of the **Love Bank.** I use it to explain how their love was created and what they did to destroy it.

> Only when your intent inspires acts of care that actually cause your spouse to be happy can it save your marriage.

There is a Love Bank inside each one of us. Every person we know has an account in our Love Bank and it keeps an emotional record of how they treat us. If a person makes us feel good, "love units" are deposited into that person's account. The better we feel, the more love units are deposited. However, if that person makes us feel bad, our emotions withdraw love units from his or her account. The number of love units withdrawn depends on how bad we feel.

For example, if your spouse makes you breakfast in bed tomorrow morning, his or her balance in your Love Bank may rise by as many as 7 or 8 love units. However, when your spouse calls you in the afternoon to cancel dinner plans because of a deadline at work, that same balance may fall by 3 or 4 love units.

The Love Bank serves a very important role in our lives. Depending on the balances in our Love Bank, our emotions encourage us to be with people who treat us well and avoid those who hurt us. We are emotionally attracted to people with positive balances and repulsed by those with negative balances.

The emotional reactions we have toward people, whether attraction or repulsion, are not a matter of choice but are dictated by our Love Bank balances. Try "choosing" to be attracted to people with whom you associate some of your worst experiences—it's almost impossible. Or try to feel repulsed by those associated with your best feelings—again, not easy. You do not decide whom you will like or dislike. It's a person's association with your feelings—whether he or she has made Love Bank deposits or withdrawals—that determines your emotional reactions to the person.

> **The Love Bank**
>
> The way our emotions keep track of how people treat us. Good experiences deposit love units, leading us to like or even love a person. Bad experiences withdraw love units, leading us to dislike or even hate a person.

We like those with positive Love Bank balances and dislike those with negative balances. But if an account is large enough to reach a certain threshold, a very special emotional reaction is triggered—romantic love. We no longer simply like the person—we are *in love*. And as I have already mentioned, being in love is a feeling of incredible attraction to someone of the opposite sex.

The feeling of love is the way our emotions encourage us to spend a great deal of time with someone who has the ability to take especially good care of us—someone who is effective in making us very happy and also knows how to avoid making us unhappy. We want to spend time with someone we like, and, by giving us the feeling of romantic love, our emotions inject added motivation. We find ourselves not only *wanting* to be with the person, but *craving* time with that person. When we are together, we feel fulfilled; and when apart, we feel lonely and incomplete. So the feeling of love is usually effective not only in drawing people together for significant amounts of time but also in encouraging them to spend their entire lives together.

But our emotions give us more than just a feeling of love. When they identify someone who makes us happy, they also motivate us to reciprocate by making that person happy. In other words, we are motivated to give caring love. And it seems almost effortless for us to do what makes the one we love the happiest.

Have you ever noticed that when you are in love, you seem instinctively affectionate, conversant, admiring, and willing to make love? That's because your emotions want you to keep that person around, so they give you instincts to help you make that person happy. If your efforts are effective, they trigger his or her feeling of love for you. The "look of love" not only communicates our feeling of love for someone but also reflects our instinct to do whatever it takes to make that person happy.

But what goes up can usually come down, and Love Bank balances are no exception. As almost every married couple has discovered, the feeling of romantic love is much more fragile than they may have originally thought. And if Love Bank balances drop below the romantic-love threshold, a couple not only loses their feeling of passion for each other, but they lose their instinct to make each other happy. What was once effortless now becomes awkward and even repulsive. Instead of the look of love, couples have the look of apathy. And without love, a husband and wife no longer want to spend their lives together. Instead, they start thinking of divorce, or at least living most of their lives apart from one another.

> The "look of love" not only communicates our feeling of love for someone but also reflects our instinct to do whatever it takes to make that person happy.

It should be obvious to you by now that the Love Bank is an extremely important concept in marriage. If you want your instincts and emotions to support your marriage, your Love Bank accounts must remain above the romantic-love threshold. But how can you keep your balances in each other's Love Bank that high? And what can you do if they have already fallen below that threshold?

> **If you want your instincts and emotions to support your marriage, your Love Bank accounts must remain above the romantic-love threshold.**

I've worked long and hard to find answers to these questions, because the answers hold the key to saving marriages. Without love, spouses are very poorly motivated to remain married for life, but with the restoration of love and its accompanying instinct to be together, the threat of divorce is overcome. Marriages are saved when the feeling of love is restored.

If you want to make Love Bank deposits and avoid making withdrawals, you must change your behavior. And to do that, you need to know how behavior forms and what you can do to change it.

To help you gain control over your behavior so that you make Love Bank deposits and avoid making Love Bank withdrawals, I will introduce you to your instincts and habits.

Key Principles

- There are two kinds of love in marriage—romantic love and caring love. Romantic love is the feeling of being in love—finding someone irresistible. Caring love is a decision to try to do what you can to make someone happy—a willingness and effort to care for someone.

- Each of us has a Love Bank that keeps track of how others treat us. When they treat us well, their balance rises; when they treat us poorly, it falls.

- Depending on our Love Bank balances, our emotions encourage us to be with certain people and discourage us from being with other people. When someone's balance in our Love Bank is high, we are attracted to that person. When it is very high, the feeling of romantic love is triggered. But when someone has a negative balance, we find that person unattractive or even repulsive.

- If you and your spouse want to trigger the feeling of romantic love in each other, you must make as many Love Bank deposits as possible and avoid withdrawals.

24

Thinking It Through

1. What were some of the most important reasons you married your spouse? Would you have married if you had not been in love?

2. How were you depositing love units into each other's Love Banks before you were married?

3. Does your care for your spouse deposit love units? Does your spouse's care for you deposit love units? In other words, is the care that you show each other effective in making each other happy?

chapter three

INSTINCTS AND
HABITS

Almost everything you do affects your spouse, sometimes very subtly and sometimes not so subtly. But whatever it is, it's making either Love Bank deposits or withdrawals. So if you want to make more Love Bank deposits and fewer withdrawals, something has to change. And that something is your behavior.

Why do you do what you do and how can you change what you do? Reflect for a moment on what happens when you first wake up in the morning. If you are at all like me, you go through a routine that is fairly predictable from morning to morning. Granted, there is always the possibility that something can throw off your routine. But if conditions remain normal, you do many of the same things every morning.

Next, reflect on how much thought you give to what you do. Chances are, when you take your shower, get dressed, eat your breakfast, and brush your teeth, you are not thinking much about what you are doing. You are probably thinking about the challenges of the day, what you did yesterday, events described in the newspaper you are reading, or you may simply be daydreaming.

The way you take your shower, dress yourself, eat your breakfast, and brush your teeth doesn't really require much thought—you do these things automatically. This isn't true only because you're half awake. It's actually a fairly accurate description of the way you go about most of your daily activities. In other words, you don't give much thought to most of what you do throughout the day. That's because just about everything you do is driven by instincts and habits. These are automatic, almost effortless, patterns of behavior that are neither intentional nor planned.

Not a Choice

Most people think that they *choose* to do whatever it is they do. Whether it's taking a shower in the morning or watching TV in the evening, people usually think that they are making a conscious and deliberate choice. If they so chose, they could take a shower a different way every morning. A change in behavior, they think, is as simple as making a decision to change.

> The vast majority of what a person does is driven by instincts and habits.

But many of us who have studied human behavior scientifically, and have tried to help people change their behavior, know differently. We know that the vast majority of what a person does is driven by instincts and habits—ways of behaving that are automatic and almost effortless.

These behaviors, of course, have an impact on the people around us. So if you want to make Love Bank deposits and avoid withdrawals, pay close attention to this subject. If you don't understand how to control your instincts and habits, they can control you and destroy the love you and your spouse have for each other.

> **Instincts**
> Behavioral patterns that do not seem to be learned. They occur in almost finished form the first time they are triggered.

You were born with instincts that are there to help you survive. Instincts are behavioral patterns that do not seem to be learned. They occur in almost finished form the first time they are triggered. It's obvious that babies have a variety of instincts because most of them do many of the same things, such as sucking their thumbs, that no one taught them how to do. But even as adults, we carry more instinctive behavior with us than we realize. And many of these instincts can make or break marriages.

Habits are different from instincts because they are behavioral patterns that are obviously learned. Typing is a good example of a habit. Without practice, you could never have walked up to a typewriter for the first time and started typing 90 words a minute. And that's what creates habits—practice. A habit is a behavioral pattern that becomes automatic and almost effortless when repeated often enough. And if certain conditions are present when you are learning the behavior (a particular room, for example), eventually those conditions will tend to trigger the habit or make it easier to perform.

For those who take a shower every morning, the shower is usually a series of habits. The way the shower is taken follows almost the same sequence every morning, and it is done with little thought or effort. But if you have an injury that forces you to take a shower differently, you will see immediately how difficult it is to shower without following your habit. Every part of your morning shower will seem awkward and uncomfortable. That's because you are not following your habit in taking your shower—instead, you are actually choosing to do everything you do, and that takes effort.

> **Habits**
> Behavioral patterns that become automatic and almost effortless when repeated often enough.

Granted, most of your habits started out as choices. When you took your first shower, very little of what you did was determined by habits. Almost every aspect of washing yourself was carefully thought through. But the more showers you took, the more your choices became habits until you got into a routine so that you had very few choices to make.

The same is true of typing. When you first started to type, you made choices about which key to press with which finger. But eventually, your typing was not driven by conscious choices each time you made a keystroke. It had become a habit.

Undoubtedly, this is not a new insight to you. For years you have understood how manual skills are learned through repetition. You already know that you learn to type by repeating correct keystrokes until you eventually type without thinking of your keystrokes. When that happens, typing has become a habit, and you tend to type best in a location and under conditions where you do it most often.

What may be a somewhat new and crucial insight for you is that other habits, such as complex social skills, are also learned by repeating certain behavior. Conversation, for example, is perfected through considerable practice, as is affection, admiration, and even honesty. When you talk to your spouse, you draw on a large reservoir of habits that help you express yourself smoothly and effortlessly. But if for some reason your conversational skill needs developing, you must create an assortment of new habits, each of them taking time and practice to develop. A simple choice to talk to your spouse differently may get you started on the right path, but at first it will seem awkward and contrived. Only after you practice the new and improved way of talking will it eventually become smooth and effortless.

We can eliminate certain habits when we discover that they do us more harm than good, and we can substitute better habits.

When I was a freshman in college, I was awed by the seniors who seemed to have it all together. My conversations with them usually left me feeling very inadequate. But when I became a senior myself, I was struck by how communicationally challenged freshmen had become. They seemed to be coming out of high school with no ability to talk whatsoever. They could hardly finish a sentence properly.

What had happened, of course, was that my own verbal skills had improved. By practicing those skills in college, I had become one of those smooth-talking seniors.

You won't have to attend college to learn how to talk with your spouse. But you will need to discover what your spouse likes to talk about and how your spouse wants you to talk to him or her. From that point on, all it takes is practice to eventually do something that makes huge Love Bank deposits—and you will be doing it almost effortlessly.

Some habits, such as effective conversation, make Love Bank deposits. But others, such as angry outbursts, make substantial withdrawals. These inappropriate habits may have been first created as valid solutions to certain problems. For example, an angry outburst may have been useful to get your mother's attention when you were an infant. But in marriage inappropriate habits usually don't get the job done, and they can ruin your love for each other.

This is where our intelligence comes in handy. We can eliminate certain habits when we discover that they do us more harm than good, and we can substitute better habits.

Habits Multiply Love Bank Deposits and Withdrawals

In my study of what it takes to build Love Bank accounts, I learned that habits are more important than isolated instances of behavior that have not yet become habits. Habits that deposit love units build very large Love Bank balances because the habits are repeated over and over almost effortlessly. Isolated behavior, on the other hand, may deposit some love units but usually doesn't affect the Love Bank very much because it isn't often repeated. In the same way, habits that withdraw love units tend to destroy Love Bank balances because they are repeated almost effortlessly.

> **Get into the habit of meeting each other's most important emotional needs and avoid habits that make each other unhappy.**

So I encourage you to get into the *habit* of meeting each other's most important emotional needs and *avoid habits* that make each other unhappy. A simple commitment to meet each other's emotional needs or to avoid hurting each other is a good place to start. But that commitment must lead to a change in behavior, and those changes must be practiced until they become habits if you expect to create a marriage that is consistently enjoyable.

As I mentioned at the beginning of this chapter, most of your behavior is not determined by choices. It is determined by instincts and habits. But choices are where you must begin if you want to change your habits. Love Bank balances will improve in your marriage only when your choices direct you to create new habits. So in the remaining pages of this book, I will be encouraging you to change your habits. Your new habits will not only build your Love

Bank balances beyond the romantic love threshold, they will also keep those balances high, because what you do for each other will become almost effortless.

How This Book Can Save Your Marriage

I've written this book to show you how to restore and sustain romantic love. The general principle is simple: You and your spouse must make as many deposits as possible into each other's Love Bank and avoid making withdrawals if you want a happy and fulfilling marriage. The next two parts of this book, How to Make Love Bank Deposits and How to Avoid Love Bank Withdrawals, will show you how to achieve each of these crucial objectives.

But there is a third objective in marriage that must also be addressed if you are to be happy. I mentioned earlier that clear communication and effective conflict resolution are not enough to save marriages, but they should not be neglected. So in the last part of this book, How to Negotiate in Marriage, I will show you how to communicate clearly and resolve your conflicts effectively with Love Bank balances in mind.

These three parts of this book are not in order of importance. I could have started with the part on negotiating or the part on how to avoid Love Bank withdrawals. That's because they are equally important, and you will need to learn the material in all three parts if you want to fall in love and stay in love. Neglecting any one of them will create trouble for you. So I encourage you to read this book in its entirety.

However, you may need to read the three parts in a different order than they are presented here. If you and your spouse find yourselves arguing so much that your time together is downright intolerable or if you are not even speaking to each other, I suggest you read part 2 last. In other words, when you finish this part, go right to parts 3 and 4 and then finish this book by going back to part 2.

Key Principles

- Almost all behavior is in the form of instincts and habits. In other words, most of what you do tends to be automatic, almost effortless, and not intentional or planned.
- An instinct is a behavioral pattern that does not seem to be learned. It occurs in almost finished form the first time it is triggered.
- A habit is a behavioral pattern that becomes automatic and almost effortless when repeated often enough.
- Habits and instincts multiply deposits into and withdrawals from the Love Bank because they are repeated almost effortlessly.

Thinking It Through

1. What are some examples of your instincts? Do they deposit love units in or withdraw love units from your spouse's Love Bank?
2. What are some examples of your habits? Do they deposit love units in or withdraw love units from your spouse's Love Bank?
3. Have you tried to change some of your habits to improve your marriage? If so, how did you go about doing it? Were you successful?

part two

HOW TO MAKE LOVE BANK DEPOSITS

chapter four

LEARNING TO
CARE
FOR EACH OTHER

One of the most astonishing enigmas I encounter in counseling is the way people use the word *care,* especially when they are having an affair. Almost invariably, wayward spouses explain that they still care about the betrayed spouse. But if that's how they act when they care, I'd hate to see how they act when they don't care!

What these people really mean is that they are somewhat concerned about their tormented spouse and hope that he or she will somehow be happy in life. Yet they are unwilling to do anything to make that person happy. In fact they are unwilling to stop doing what makes him or her miserable.

> **Caring Love**
> A decision to try to do what you can to make your spouse happy—a willingness and effort to care for your spouse.

In chapter 2, I defined **caring love,** the second kind of love, as a willingness and effort to try to make someone happy. But the way unfaithful spouses usually use the term when applied to their betrayed spouse is a cruel hoax. The word may lead the "cared for" person to think that his or her best interests are being promoted, but that's far from the truth. In fact, in the case of an affair, the opposite is the case. Their interests are being totally ignored.

It isn't that those having an affair do not know how to care. They care for their lover in a most extraordinary way. In fact my goal is to help you care for your spouse with the same quality and intensity that unfaithful spouses usually care for their lover. They know how to care, all right. But when an unfaithful spouse tells me that he or she cares about the betrayed spouse, it distorts the true meaning of the word.

Think of *care* in the context of caring for your children. *Care* doesn't simply mean you hope your children turn out to be successful and happy. *Care* means much more than that. It means you are actually doing something to see to it that your children are successful and happy. Child care is watching over them to ensure their safety and happiness, not just hoping that they will be all right as you drive off leaving them alone to fend for themselves.

The same meaning of *care* applies in marriage. If you are effective in caring, you are doing what it takes to make your spouse happy. And when you are very effective in caring, he or she will experience the first meaning of love—romantic love. Your spouse will be *in love* with you because your effort to care deposits so many love units.

> **Care is your willingness to try to make each other happy and your effort that puts your willingness into action.**

So when I use the word *care* I use it to indicate what people are willing to *do* for each other. *Care* is your willingness to try to make each other happy and your effort that puts your willingness into action. When you say you care for each other, you are promising to enhance the quality and enjoyment of each other's life, and you are doing something to try to achieve that objective.

You decided to marry because you found each other irresistible and you simply could not imagine living without each other. It's the Love Bank's fault. Before you married, you managed to deposit so many love units into each other's Love Bank that you triggered the inevitable reaction of romantic love. That feeling of love encouraged you to spend the rest of your lives together. But it was your care that created the feeling of love you had for each other. By caring, you deposited huge sums of love units into your Love Banks.

Since the feeling of love had so much to do with your decision to marry, and caring love had so much to do with your feeling of love, you need to fully understand how and when caring love leads to romantic love. As I mentioned earlier, love is not a mystery. It's a predictable emotional reaction. Care helps create the feeling of love.

The Art of Caring

Some of us are naturally talented in making others feel good, but most of us have had to learn how to do it through trial and error. Fortunately, as children, we were usually quick to let others know how they were affecting us. When they did something we liked, they became our friends, and when they upset us, they became our enemies. But enemies could become friends and vice versa between recess and lunch. So as children we could redeem ourselves rather quickly if we had made a social blunder.

By the time we entered adolescence, most of us had figured out social etiquette well enough to attract friends who remained friends for weeks, or even months, at a time. Some of these friends were of the opposite sex, and that added a new dimension to the meaning of friendship.

We discovered that at least some of our opposite-sex friends gave us feelings that we had never felt before—better than any we had ever experienced. We were used to friends making us feel good, but this was fantastic! Imagine, me, talking to some girl on the telephone for hours. I never did that with my best friend, Steve. So why did I want to do it with Joyce? Because it felt so good just to talk to her. And she apparently felt the same way talking to me. We were depositing love units into each other's Love Banks at an unprecedented rate.

Just as I could make Joyce very happy, though, I could also upset her. I discovered that what worked well for my same-sex friends did not always find approval with my opposite-sex friends. Things that never bothered Steve bothered Joyce. And I seemed to bother Joyce almost effortlessly.

I played practical jokes on her that drove her nuts, and my jokes withdrew all the love units from her Love Bank that I had deposited when we talked on the telephone. That taught me a very important lesson: If I wanted Joyce to stay in love with me, I had to avoid wrecking it all with my thoughtlessness.

> **If I wanted Joyce to stay in love with me, I had to avoid wrecking it all with my thoughtlessness.**

Still, Joyce's love for me and my love for her were not a result of our making each other feel merely good. It was the result of our making each other feel sensational. The romantic love threshold was broken through because we had both deposited an extraordinary number of love units.

The most sought-after girls in my high school were those who knew how to make guys feel terrific every time they were together. Quite frankly, their physical appearance usually had a lot to do with it, but they also knew how to show guys the kind of attention that made the girls particularly attractive.

And the boys who were the most popular among the girls were those who knew how to make girls feel great—to sweep them off their feet. Those guys had learned the art of caring, the art of depositing love units. Those of us who were not among the most popular would often try to copy what we thought the popular boys were doing. Sometimes it worked and sometimes it didn't.

Care is definitely an art. You and your spouse were artful enough to fall in love with each other. Try to remember what you did to deposit all those love units. What caused such a large deposit that you broke through the romantic-love threshold and fell in love? If you want to be as much in love now as you were then, you must have a correct answer to that question. And I will give you that answer. But first, I must explain something that has a great deal to do with Love Bank deposits—emotional needs.

What Is an Emotional Need?

We all know about physical needs, such as the need for food, water, oxygen, warmth, and so forth. These are essential to our survival, and with them our bodies thrive. Without them, we die.

There is another kind of need that all of us have—emotional needs. We don't necessarily die when these needs are not met but sometimes we wish we would. An emotional need is a craving that, when satisfied, makes us feel happy and fulfilled and, when unsatisfied, makes us feel unhappy and frustrated.

Most physical needs are also emotional needs. Physical deprivation often leads to emotional craving, and physical satisfaction to emotional contentment. Food is a good example. When we are hungry, a physical need for food is accompanied by an emotional craving for food. The same thing is true of water.

But not every physical need is also an emotional need. For example, we need oxygen but we don't have an emotional reaction every time the need is not met. We can breathe, say, helium instead of oxygen and feel emotionally okay right up to the moment we pass out. Oxygen is a physical need without an emotional component.

On the other hand, most emotional needs are not physical needs. What makes us feel good in life often has nothing to do with our physical well-being. In fact there are many emotional needs that, when met, actually threaten our physical health. For example, we put our health at risk when we yield to the emotional craving for certain drugs and alcohol.

> **Emotional Need**
>
> A craving that, when satisfied, makes us feel happy and fulfilled and, when unsatisfied, makes us feel unhappy and frustrated.

There are thousands of emotional needs—a need for birthday parties (or at least birthday presents), peanut butter sandwiches, *Monday Night Football* . . . I could go on and on. Whenever one of our emotional needs is met, we feel good, and when it's unmet, we feel frustrated. Try telling a football fan that he can't watch football this week, and you get a taste of how emotional needs affect people.

It's easy to determine your own emotional needs. All you must do is pay attention to what you enjoy the most when you have it, and miss the most when you don't. If you feel good when someone does something for you, and you feel frustrated when they don't, that something is an emotional need.

But not all emotional needs are created equal. When some are met, you feel just comfortable—they make small Love Bank deposits. There are others, however, that, when met, can make you feel downright euphoric. In fact they make you so happy that you're likely to fall in love with whoever meets them. I call those needs our **most important emotional needs** because, when they are met, the largest of all Love Bank deposits are made. And these are the very same emotional needs that a husband and wife expect each other to meet in marriage.

Care and Emotional Needs

In marriage *care* is meeting the most important emotional needs. When a husband and wife come to me for help, I want them to make the largest deposits possible into each other's Love Banks. So my first goal is to help them identify their most important emotional needs—what each of them can do for the other that will make them the happiest and most contented. And once those needs are identified, I help them learn to become experts at meeting those emotional needs. If all goes well, they begin making large Love Bank deposits and eventually they are in love with each other.

> **When our most important emotional needs are met, the largest of all Love Bank deposits are made.**

When I first started using this approach to saving marriages, I didn't know what made people the happiest in marriage. I didn't know which emotional needs would be the most important. So I had to ask hundreds of men and women this question: "What could your spouse do for you that would make you the happiest?"

As spouses explained to me what they wanted most, I classified their desires into emotional-need categories. And almost all those I interviewed described one or more of the same ten emotional needs as important to them: admiration, affection, conversation, domestic support, family commitment, financial support, honesty and openness, physical attractiveness, recreational companionship, and sexual fulfillment.

But I made another discovery that helped me understand the reason husbands and wives tended *not* to meet each other's emotional needs. Whenever I asked couples to list their needs according to their priority, men would list them one way and women a completely different way. Of the top ten emotional needs, the five listed as most important by men were usually the five least important for women, and vice versa.

What a revolutionary insight! No wonder husbands and wives have so much difficulty meeting each other's needs! They lack empathy. What they appreciate the most, their spouses appreciate the least! They follow the Golden Rule—do for your spouse what you would want your spouse to do for you. But since their needs are not always the same, their efforts are unappreciated. If spouses are to meet each other's needs, they must do for each other what they don't necessarily appreciate themselves.

> If spouses are to meet each other's needs, they must do for each other what they don't necessarily appreciate themselves.

Pay close attention to this next point I am about to make, because it is one of the most misunderstood aspects of my entire program. Everyone is unique. While men on average pick a particular five emotional needs as their most important and women on average pick another five, **any particular man or woman can pick various combinations of the ten.** So even though I have discovered the most important emotional needs of the average man and woman, I don't know the emotional needs of any particular husband or wife. In other words, I don't know what *your* emotional needs are.

This book is aimed at saving *your* marriage, not just the *average* marriage. So rather than focusing on each need as characteristically male or female, I encourage you to discover the needs that are unique to you and your spouse. Then your lists of important emotional needs will reflect what both of you appreciate the most. When you meet those needs for each other, the mutual feeling of love will be triggered.

I have provided the Emotional Needs Questionnaire (appendix B) so that you can identify your most important emotional needs and those of your spouse. But before you fill out the questionnaire, let me describe each of the ten basic emotional needs so that you will be able to make an intelligent decision as to which are most important to you. The next two chapters define and describe these ten emotional needs.

When you have identified your most important emotional needs, you will know what to do to make each other happy. You will know how to care for each other.

Key Principles

- *Care* doesn't simply mean you hope your spouse will be happy. *Care* means much more than that. It means you are actually doing something to see to it that your spouse *is* happy.

- An emotional need is a craving that, when satisfied, makes us feel happy and fulfilled and, when unsatisfied, makes us feel unhappy and frustrated.

- When our most important emotional needs are met, the largest of all Love Bank deposits are made.

- If spouses are to meet each other's needs, they must do for each other what they don't necessarily appreciate themselves.

Thinking It Through

1. I have defined *caring love* as your willingness to try to make each other happy and your effort that puts your willingness into action. Do you agree with this definition, or does *caring love* have some other meaning for you?

2. What are you and your spouse doing now to try to make each other happy?

3. When you were dating before marriage, what did you do for each other that was particularly effective in making each other happy? In other words, what was it that each of you did that deposited the most love units?

4. Do you think your willingness and effort to make each other happy has increased or decreased since you were married? Why?

HIS MOST IMPORTANT EMOTIONAL NEEDS

Do you know yourself well enough to list your most important emotional needs? What makes you the happiest when you have it and the most frustrated when you do not have it? What is it about someone that is most likely to trigger your feeling of romantic love?

Most people have not given this much thought and, if forced to make up a list, would not know where to begin. But it's very important that you understand your emotional needs, not only for your sake but also for your spouse's sake. If he or she is to put time and energy into becoming an expert at meeting your needs, you'd better be sure you have identified the right needs. And it's also important for you to understand your spouse's emotional needs so that you too can put your effort in the right places.

To help you identify your most important emotional needs, I will describe ten that are common to most couples. My list of needs may not include all the needs that are important to you. Ambition is a good example of a need that I have excluded from my list of ten. Some people gain tremendous pleasure from the ambition of their spouse. As long as their spouse continues to achieve important objectives, love units keep pouring in. I have found this need to be so uncommon that it did not make my final cut. In your case, however, it may make the cut, and you may want to include it on your list of most important emotional needs. If something gives you enough pleasure to trigger your feeling of love, and it's not on my list of ten needs, be sure to let your spouse know about it.

For most of us, the ten needs that I describe cover the most important needs of most people. In this chapter I will describe the five emotional needs that tend to be chosen by men as most important. And then in the next chapter, I will describe the five needs that women tend to identify as most important.

Sexual Fulfillment

When you married, you and your spouse both promised to be faithful to each other for life. This means that you agreed to be each other's only sexual partner "until death do us part." You made this commitment because you trusted each other to meet your sexual needs, to be sexually available and responsive to each other. The need for sex, then, is a very exclusive need, and if you have this need, you will be very dependent on your spouse to meet it for you. You have no other ethical choices.

> **Sexual Fulfillment**
>
> If you tend to feel happy and contented when you make love, and you feel frustrated when you don't make love often enough or in the way you want to make love, you have a need for sexual fulfillment.

In most marriages, one spouse, usually the husband, has a much greater need for sex than the other. This tends to create a significant conflict if his need is not being met as often as he would like or in the way he would like it to be met. That's why it is very important for you and your spouse to understand which one of you has the greatest need for sex and how you can effectively meet that need for each other. Without that understanding and skill, you are likely to join the majority of marriages in which the need for sex is not being adequately addressed.

Most people know whether or not they have a need for sex, but in case there is any uncertainty, I will point out some of the most obvious characteristics.

A sexual need usually predates your relationship with each other and is somewhat independent of your relationship. While you may have discovered a deep desire to make love to your spouse since you've been in love, it isn't quite the same thing as a sexual need. Wanting to make love when you are in love is sometimes merely a reflection of wanting to be emotionally and physically close.

> **A sexual need usually predates your relationship with each other and is somewhat independent of your relationship.**

Sexual fantasies are usually a dead giveaway for a sexual need. If you tend to daydream about what it would be like having your sexual need met in the most fulfilling ways, you probably have a sexual need. The more often this fantasy is employed, the greater your need. And the way your sexual need is met in your fantasy is usually a good indicator of your sexual predisposition and orientation.

The need for sex and the need for affection, which I will describe in the next chapter, are often confused with each other. To understand the difference, think of it this way: Affection is an act of love (hugging, kissing, hand-holding) that is nonsexual and can be shared with friends, relatives, children, and even pets with absolutely no sexual intent. If your acts of affection tend to have a sexual motive, they reveal your need for sex, not your need for affection.

If you tend to feel happy and contented when you make love, and you feel frustrated when you don't make love often enough or in the way you want to make love, you have a need for sexual fulfillment.

Recreational Companionship

Before you and your spouse were married, chances are pretty good that you planned your dates around your favorite recreational activities. If recreational companionship is one of the most important emotional needs of you or your spouse, doing things together may have deposited enough love units in your Love Banks to trigger romantic love. And since you wanted your relationship to flourish, you probably chose activities that you both enjoyed.

But you may have made the mistake of doing whatever the one with the greatest need for recreational companionship wanted to do. That's what happened to my wife, Joyce, and me. She was willing to join me in all of the recreational activities I liked the most—right up to the day we were married. But after marriage, she announced that she would be joining me only in activities that she also enjoyed. And it turned out that she shared very few of my recreational interests.

Most couples whose marriages begin the way mine did make a crucial mistake—they go their separate ways. He joins his friends in recreational activities he enjoys most and leaves his wife to find her own recreational companions for activities that interest her. That's a formula for marital disaster. If someone else of the opposite sex joins either of you in your favorite recreational activities, you are at risk of falling in love with that person. Besides, if you are not together when you are enjoying yourselves the most, you are squandering an opportunity to deposit love units.

> If someone else of the opposite sex joins either of you in your favorite recreational activities, you are at risk of falling in love with that person.

Fortunately, Joyce and I took the path that led to marital fulfillment. We exchanged the old activities that only I enjoyed for new activities that we both enjoyed. We remained each other's favorite recreational companion after marriage even though most of our recreational activities changed. And it's a good thing, because recreational companionship is definitely one of my most important emotional needs.

The need for recreational companionship combines two needs into one. First, there is the need to be engaged in recreational activities, and, second, there is the need to have a companion. To determine if you have this need, first ask yourself if you have a craving for certain recreational activities. Then ask yourself if the activities require a companion for fulfillment. If recreational activities are important to you, and someone else must join you for them to be fulfilling, include recreational companionship on your list of emotional needs.

Think about it for a moment in terms of the Love Bank. How much do you enjoy these activities, and how many love units would your spouse be depositing whenever you enjoyed them together? What a waste it would be if someone else got credit for all those love units! And if it was someone of the opposite sex, it would be downright dangerous.

Who should get credit for all those love units? The one you should love the most, your spouse. That's precisely why I encourage couples to be each other's favorite recreational companion. It's one of the simplest ways to deposit love units.

Physical Attractiveness

For many, physical attractiveness can be one of the greatest sources of love units. If you have this need, an attractive person will not only get your attention but may distract you from whatever it was you were doing. In fact that's what may have first drawn you to your spouse—his or her physical attractiveness.

There are some who consider this need temporary and important only in the beginning of a relationship. Some feel that after a couple gets to know each other better, physical attractiveness should take a backseat to deeper

> **Physical Attractiveness**
>
> If the attractiveness of your spouse makes you feel great and loss of that attractiveness would make you feel very frustrated, you should include physical attractiveness on your list of important emotional needs.

and more intimate needs. I've even heard some suggest that those with a need for physical attractiveness are immature or spiritually weak—even subhuman!

But I don't judge important emotional needs, and I don't think you should either. The question you should ask is, What need, when met, deposits the most love units? If it's physical attractiveness, it should not be ignored. For many, the need for physical attractiveness is present not only at the beginning of a relationship but throughout marriage, and love units are deposited whenever the spouse is seen—if he or she is physically attractive.

Among the various aspects of physical attractiveness, weight generally gets the most attention. Almost all of the complaints I hear regarding a spouse's loss of physical attractiveness relate to being overweight. And when diet and exercise bring the spouse back to a healthy size, physical attractiveness almost always returns. However, choice of clothing, hairstyle, makeup, and personal hygiene also come together to make a person attractive.

Since attractiveness is usually in the eye of the beholder, you are the ultimate judge of what is attractive to you. If the attractiveness of your spouse makes you feel great and loss of that attractiveness would make you feel very frustrated, you should include physical attractiveness on your list of important emotional needs.

Admiration

If you have the need for admiration, you may have fallen in love with your spouse partly because of his or her compliments to you. Some people just love to be told that they are appreciated. Your spouse may also have been careful not to criticize you, because criticism may hurt you deeply if you have this need.

> **Admiration**
>
> If you are easily affected by your spouse's words of admiration or criticism, add admiration to your list of important emotional needs.

Many of us have a deep desire to be respected, valued, and appreciated. We need to be affirmed clearly and often. There's nothing wrong with feeling that way. Even God wants us to appreciate him.

Admiration is one of the easiest needs to meet. Just a word of appreciation, and presto, you've just made somebody's day. On the other hand, it's also easy to be critical. A trivial word of rebuke can ruin the day for some people and withdraw love units at an alarming rate.

Your spouse may have the power to build up or deplete his or her account in your Love Bank with just a few words of admiration or criticism. If you can be affected that easily, be sure to add admiration to your list of important emotional needs.

Domestic Support

Domestic support involves the creation of a peaceful and well-managed home environment. It includes cooking meals, washing dishes, washing and ironing clothes, housecleaning and child care. If you have the need for domestic support, you feel very fulfilled when your spouse does some of these things, and when they are not done, you feel very annoyed.

The need for domestic support is a time bomb. When a couple is first married, it often seems irrelevant, a throwback to more primitive times. But for many couples, the need explodes after a few years of marriage, surprising both spouses.

> **Domestic Support**
>
> If you find yourself very appreciative of your spouse's cooking, cleaning, and child care and very frustrated when these things are not done, make sure that domestic support is on your list of emotional needs.

In earlier generations, it was assumed that all husbands had this need and all wives would naturally meet it. Times have changed, and needs have changed along with them. Now, many of the men I counsel would rather have their wives meet other, more important emotional needs, such as affection or conversation, needs that have traditionally been more characteristic of women. And many women, especially career women, find themselves gaining a great deal of pleasure when their husbands create a peaceful and well-managed home environment for them. But on average, men still express the need for domestic support more often than women.

Marriage usually begins with a willingness of both spouses to share domestic responsibilities. Newlyweds commonly wash dishes together, make the bed together, and divide many household tasks. The groom welcomes the help he gets from his wife, helping him do what he's been doing alone as a bachelor. At this point in marriage, neither of them would identify domestic support as an important emotional need. But the time bomb is ticking.

When does the need for domestic support explode? When the children arrive! Children create huge needs—both a greater need for income and greater domestic responsibilities. The previous division of labor is now obsolete, and both spouses must take on new responsibilities.

If you do not have children, you may have no need at all for domestic support. But if you find yourself very appreciative of your spouse's cooking, cleaning, and child care, and very frustrated when these things are not done, make sure that domestic support is on your list of emotional needs.

The Irresistible Wife

The five emotional needs that I have identified in this chapter are the ones given the highest priority by the average man. If your wife met these needs for you, chances are very good that you would find her irresistible.

1. *Sexual fulfillment.* Your wife meets this need by being a terrific sexual partner for you. She studies her own sexual response to recognize and understand what brings the best out in her sexually; then she shares that information with you, and together you learn to have a sexual relationship that is as frequent as you want and enjoyable for both of you.

2. *Recreational companionship.* Your wife develops an interest in the recreational activities that you enjoy the most and tries to become proficient at them. If she finds that she cannot enjoy them, she encourages you to consider other activities that you can enjoy together. She is your favorite recreational companion, and you associate her with your most enjoyable moments of relaxation.

3. *Physical attractiveness*. Your wife keeps herself physically fit with diet and exercise, and she wears her hair, makeup, and clothes in a way that you find attractive and tasteful. You are attracted to her in private and proud of her in public.

4. *Admiration*. Your wife understands and appreciates you more than anyone else does. She reminds you of your value and achievements and helps you maintain self-confidence. She avoids criticizing you. She is proud of you, not out of duty but from a profound respect for the man she chose to marry.

5. *Domestic support*. Your wife creates a home environment that offers you a refuge from the stresses of life. She manages the household responsibilities in a way that encourages you to spend time at home enjoying your family.

Only you can determine if these are your most important emotional needs. When these needs are met, are you so happy that you tend to fall in love with whoever meets them? Perhaps this list does not include your most important emotional needs at all. You may find that one or more of the needs I describe in the next chapter are more important to you.

Your wife may find that some of the needs I've just described are so important to her that she would find you irresistible if you met them for her. If that's the case, you should know about them. So far I have described only half of the ten most important emotional needs, so let's get to the rest of them before you make up your final list.

Key Principles

- You have a need for sexual fulfillment if you tend to feel happy and contented when you make love, and you feel frustrated when you don't make love often enough or in the way you want to make love.

- You have a need for recreational companionship if you enjoy recreational activities with a companion and are frustrated when you don't spend enough of your leisure time engaged in recreational activities.

• You have a need for physical attractiveness if the attractiveness of your spouse makes you feel great and the loss of that attractiveness would make you feel very frustrated.

• You have a need for admiration if words of admiration make you feel fulfilled and words of criticism tend to crush you.

• You have a need for domestic support if your spouse's cooking, cleaning, and child care make you very happy, and when they are not done, you feel very frustrated.

Thinking It Through

1. Do you feel dependent on your spouse to meet your need for sex? Do you recognize your spouse's dependence on you? How are you presently addressing that dependency?

2. Do you agree with me that the need for sex is a very exclusive need? How far do you want each other to carry that exclusivity? For example, how do you feel about each other's use of pornography?

3. When you were dating, did you engage in your most enjoyable recreational activities together? Now that you are married, are you still spending your recreational time together? If not, why not?

4. Do you feel that physical attractiveness is a legitimate need in marriage? In other words, do you feel that you should look your best for each other as an act of care?

5. Do you express admiration for each other often enough? How sensitive are you to each other's criticism? Is that sensitivity evidence of your need for admiration?

6. Are you having conflicts over the division of household responsibilities? How do you feel about doing some household tasks as a way to meet your spouse's emotional needs?

7. Does my "irresistible wife" sound attractive (to the husband) and realistic (to the wife)?

chapter six

HER MOST IMPORTANT EMOTIONAL NEEDS

When I began asking husbands and wives to tell me what would make them the happiest, I didn't try to second-guess them. I took their word for it, and then tried to encourage them to meet each other's needs. After several hundred couples identified their needs, the most important needs of the average husband and wife began to emerge. What struck me most was not just that the priority of needs was different for husband and wife, but rather that the categories the needs fell into were different.

The needs men most often identified as most important seemed to represent some form of recreation and comfort. Sexual fulfillment, recreational companionship, physical attractiveness, domestic support, and admiration—they all fit neatly into the category of leisure pleasures. A woman, then, has the greatest opportunity to make Love Bank deposits during a man's leisure time. That's probably what dating is all about for most men—a great way to spend time after work. I know that's how it was for me before I was married.

The needs of the average woman, however, seemed to fall into a completely different category. Affection, conversation, honesty and openness, financial support, and family commitment—they all seemed to fit into the category of security. A man's efforts to provide security and fulfill a woman's trust seemed to make the most Love Bank deposits for the average woman.

> Each person is unique, and most husbands and wives will choose at least one need that does not fit the average set of five needs for their sex.

At the end of a successful date, most women feel emotionally connected with a man who has earned their trust by talking openly with them and showing his affection in nonsexual ways. Before we were married, Joyce commented on many occasions that she felt more comfortable with me than anyone she had dated. I earned her trust, and that deposited love units.

But let me reiterate. Each person is unique, and most husbands and wives will choose at least one need that does not fit the average set of five needs for their sex. So in this chapter, even though I am describing the five most important emotional needs of the average woman, most men will choose at least one of these for their list of most important emotional needs. Remember, what gives you the greatest pleasure when met and the greatest frustration when left unmet is an important emotional need for you. If it's among the following needs, be sure to add it to your list regardless of your sex.

Affection

Quite simply, affection is the expression of love. It symbolizes security, protection, comfort, and approval—vitally important ingredients in any relationship. When one spouse is affectionate to the other, the following messages are being sent. (1) You are important to me, and I will care for you and protect you; (2) I'm concerned about the problems you face and will be there for you when you need me.

> **Affection**
>
> If you feel terrific when your spouse expresses love and care for you and you feel terrible when there is not enough of it, you have the emotional need for affection.

A simple hug can say those things. When we hug our friends and relatives, we are demonstrating our care for them. And there are other ways to show our affection: a greeting card or an "I love you" note, a bouquet of flowers, holding hands, walks after dinner, back rubs, phone calls, and conversations with thoughtful and loving expressions. All can communicate affection.

Affection should send a message of care and consideration.

But don't confuse affection with sex. Affection should send a message of care and consideration. When acts commonly associated with affection, such as hugging or kissing, have a sexual motive, the message changes to what the giver wants for him or her rather than a commitment to care for the other spouse.

Affection is, for many, the essential cement of a relationship. Without it, many feel totally alienated. With it, they become emotionally bonded. If you feel terrific when your spouse expresses love and care for you and you feel terrible when there is not enough of it, you have the emotional need for affection.

Conversation

Unlike the need for sex, conversation is not an emotional need that must be met exclusively in marriage. Our need for conversation can be ethically met by almost anyone. But if it is one of your most important emotional needs, whoever meets it best will deposit so many love units, you may fall in love with that person. So if it's your need, it's crucial to your marital happiness—and protection from an affair—that your spouse be the one who meets it the best and most often.

Conversation

If you enjoy conversation in its own right and are frustrated when you haven't been able to talk for a while, consider it one of your most important emotional needs.

The need for conversation is not met by simply talking to someone. It is met when the conversation is enjoyable to both. Good conversation is characterized by the following: (1) It is used to inform and investigate each other; (2) it focuses attention on topics of mutual interest; (3) it is balanced, with both people having an equal opportunity to talk; and (4) both people give each other undivided attention when they talk to each other.

Conversation fails to meet this need when (1) demands are made; (2) disrespect is shown; (3) one or both become angry; or (4) it is used to dwell on mistakes of the past or present. Unless conversation is mutually enjoyable, a couple is better off not talking at all. An unpleasant conversation not only fails to meet the emotional need, but it also makes it less likely that there will be an opportunity to meet the need in the future. That's because we tend to prevent our spouse from meeting our needs if earlier attempts turned out to be painful to us.

> **Unless conversation is mutually enjoyable, a couple is better off not talking at all.**

Men and women do not have much difficulty talking to each other during courtship. That's a time of information gathering for both partners. Both are highly motivated to discover each other's likes and dislikes, personal background, current interests, and plans for the future. But after marriage, many women find that the man who used to spend hours with them on the telephone now seems to have lost all interest in talking to them and spends his spare time watching television or working on a project in the garage.

If your need for conversation was fulfilled during courtship, you expect it to be met after marriage. And if you fell in love because your need for conversation was met by your spouse during courtship, you risk falling out of love if that need is not met during marriage.

Do you have a craving just to talk to someone? Do you pick up the telephone just because you feel like talking? If you see conversation only as a practical necessity, primarily as a means to an end, you probably don't have much of a need for it. But if you enjoy conversation in its own right and are frustrated when you haven't been able to talk for a while, consider it one of your most important emotional needs.

Honesty and Openness

Most of us want an honest relationship with our spouse. But some people have an emotional need for honesty and openness. Honesty and openness give them a sense of security and help them become emotionally bonded to the one who meets that need.

> **Honesty and Openness**
>
> If you feel happy and fulfilled when your spouse reveals his or her most private thoughts to you and very frustrated when they are hidden from you, include honesty and openness as one of your most important emotional needs.

Those with a need for honesty and openness want accurate information about their spouse's thoughts, feelings, habits, likes, dislikes, personal history, daily activities, and plans for the future. If their spouse does not provide honest and open communication, trust is undermined and the feelings of security can eventually be destroyed. They cannot trust the signals that are being sent and feel they have no foundation on which to build a solid relationship. Instead of adjusting, they feel off balance; instead of growing together, they feel as if they are growing apart.

Honesty and openness help build compatibility in marriage. When you and your spouse openly reveal the facts of your past, your present activities, and your plans for the future, you are able to make intelligent decisions that take each other's feelings into account. And that's how you create compatibility—by making decisions that work well for both of you simultaneously.

Aside from the practical considerations of honesty and openness, the person with this need feels happy and fulfilled when the spouse reveals his or her most private thoughts and very frustrated when they are hidden. That reaction is evidence of an emotional need, and if that is the way you feel, include honesty and openness as one of your most important emotional needs.

Financial Support

People often marry for the financial security that their spouse provides them. In other words, part of the reason they marry is for money.

But there are others who marry before financial security becomes much of a consideration for them. They do not marry for money because their new spouse has none. And yet, as years go by, when they find their spouse unemployed or underemployed or squandering what money they have, they become very frustrated and unhappy. Their need for financial support seems to develop after they are married for a while, especially after children arrive.

> **Financial Support**
>
> If a person's income or wealth makes him or her more attractive to you and the lack of money makes him or her unattractive, you probably have a need for financial support.

It may be difficult for you to know how much you need financial support, especially if you were recently married or if your spouse has always been gainfully employed. But what if, before marriage, your spouse had told you not to expect any income from him or her. Would it have affected your decision to marry? Or what if your spouse could not find work, and you had to financially support him or her throughout life? Would that withdraw love units?

You may have a need for financial support if you expect your spouse to earn a living. And you definitely have that need if you do not expect to be earning a living yourself, at least during part of your marriage.

What constitutes financial support? Earning enough to buy everything you could possibly desire or earning just enough to get by? Different people would answer this differently, and the same person might answer differently in different stages of life. That's why this need can be difficult to meet—it can change over time.

Like many emotional needs, financial support is sometimes hard to talk about. As a result, many spouses have hidden expectations, assumptions, and resentments. How much money does your spouse have to earn before you feel fulfilled, and what would it take for you to feel frustrated about his or her paycheck? Your analysis will help you determine if you have a need for financial support, and if so, whether or not this need is being met.

Another point to remember is that when an emotional need is met, love units are deposited in very large numbers. In other words, if someone were to meet this need for you, might you fall in love with that person? Does a person's income or wealth make him or her more attractive to you? And are those without money unattractive? If so, you probably have a need for financial support.

Family Commitment

In addition to a greater need for income, the arrival of children may create in you the need for your spouse to become active in the moral and educational development of the children. I call that need family commitment. As is true for the need for financial support, if you don't have any children just yet, you may not sense this need. But with their arrival, a change may take place that you didn't anticipate.

Evidence of this need is a craving for your spouse's involvement in the training of your children. When he or she is helping to care for them, you feel very fulfilled, and when they are neglected, you feel very frustrated.

Family commitment is not just child care—feeding, clothing, or watching over children to keep them safe. Child care falls into the needs category of domestic support. Family commitment, on the other hand, is taking responsibility for how the children will turn

> **Family Commitment**
>
> If your spouse's participation with you in the moral and educational development of your children makes you feel fulfilled and his or her neglect of the children makes you feel very frustrated, you have a need for family commitment.

out, teaching them values, such as cooperation with and care for each other. It is spending quality time with your children to help ensure happiness and success for them as adults.

The need for family commitment is not met by just any form of child training. It is met only when the training is enthusiastically approved by you. It can all be ruined if your spouse uses training methods and objectives that violate your own standards. Your participation and agreement regarding training methods and objectives are essential before this need can be met.

We all want our children to be successful, and if you have an emotional need for family commitment, your spouse's participation in family activities will deposit so many love units that it will trigger your feeling of love for him or her. And your spouse's neglect of your children will threaten your love.

The Irresistible Husband

Most of our happiness in life comes from our relationships with others. That's because we cannot meet our most important emotional needs by ourselves—others must meet them for us. And we usually fall in love with the person who is doing the best job of meeting them. Your husband has been your greatest source of happiness, at least when you were in love with him. And he can and should be your greatest source of happiness for the rest of your lives together.

Your husband can become irresistible to you if he simply meets your most important emotional needs. For many women they are the five needs discussed in this chapter.

1. *Affection.* Your husband tells you that he loves you and cares for you with words, cards, flowers, gifts, and common courtesies. He hugs and kisses you many times a day, creating an environment of affection that clearly and repeatedly expresses his love and care for you.

> We cannot meet our most important emotional needs by ourselves—others must meet them for us.

2. *Conversation.* He sets aside time each day just to talk to you. He talks with you about events in your lives, your children, your feelings, and your plans. But whatever the topic, he avoids demands, disrespect, or anger, and he doesn't dwell on your mistakes. When he talks to you, he gives you his undivided attention and makes sure you both contribute equally to the conversation.

3. *Honesty and openness.* Your husband tells you everything about himself, leaving nothing out that might later surprise you. He describes his positive and negative feelings, events of his past, his daily schedule, and his plans for the future. He does not confuse

demands, disrespect, or anger with honesty. He is respectful whenever your opinions differ. He is also interested in knowing about your feelings, events of your past, your daily schedule, and your plans for the future.

4. *Financial support.* Your husband assumes responsibility to house, feed, and clothe your family. If his income is insufficient to provide essential support, he is willing to upgrade his skills to provide that support, without having to work long hours that would keep him from you. He encourages you to pursue a career but does not depend on your salary for basic family expenses.

5. *Family commitment.* He commits sufficient time and energy to the moral and educational development of your children. He reads to them, engages in sports with them, and takes them on frequent outings. He also reads books and attends lectures with you on the subject of child development so that you will both do a good job training your children. He discusses training methods and objectives with you until you both agree, and he does not proceed with any plan of discipline without your approval. He recognizes that the happiness and success of your children is critically important to you.

Some men may look at this list of needs and throw up their hands in despair. And it does look like a lot of work if you are not in the habit of doing any of these things. But it's not really that difficult to become an irresistible husband. All it takes is getting into habits that meet these most important emotional needs. After that, it becomes second nature.

Of course, education and training are required to develop skill at almost anything. And marriage requires basic skills for success. People take courses regularly to become experts at all sorts of things—computer programming, business management, hairstyling. Skills in marriage are even more important than any vocational skill could possibly be. That's because if you are happily married, everything you do will be easier and more inspired. But if your marriage is disappointing, it will place a burden on everything you do and value.

If you're smart, you will train yourself in what counts the most. Learn through practice to meet each other's most important emo-

Learn through
practice
to meet each other's
most important
emotional
needs at
expert level.

tional needs at expert level and then throughout your marriage keep your skills finely tuned so that you will find each other irresistible.

As I mentioned before, these five needs may not accurately reflect your (the wife's) most important needs. You may feel that some of the needs described in the last chapter mean more to you than some of the ones I've described in this chapter. The question you should ask yourself is, What makes me the happiest when I have it and makes me most frustrated when I don't have it? The answer to that question will illuminate your emotional needs.

Now that I have described all ten emotional needs, we are finally ready to identify those that are most important to you and your spouse. We will do that in the next chapter. And then you will be in a position to know where your effort will have the greatest effect on your love for each other.

Key Principles

- You have a need for affection if you feel terrific when your spouse expresses love and care for you and you feel terrible when there is not enough of it.

- You have a need for conversation if you enjoy conversation in its own right and are frustrated when you haven't been able to talk for a while.

- You have a need for honesty and openness if you feel happy and fulfilled when your spouse reveals his or her most private thoughts to you and very frustrated when they are hidden.

- You have a need for financial support if a person's income or wealth makes him or her more attractive to you and the lack of money makes him or her unattractive.

- You have a need for family commitment if your spouse's participation with you in the moral and educational development of your children will deposit so many love units that it will trigger your feeling of love for him or her and if your spouse's neglect of your children will threaten that love.

- Learn to meet each other's most important emotional needs at expert level and then throughout your marriage keep your skills finely tuned so that you will find each other irresistible.

Thinking It Through

1. Have you ever thought about affection as a need that is nonsexual? In other words, do you value affection more when your spouse does not use it as a signal for sex? If a spouse does not show affection unless it is associated with sex, it usually means that spouse has a need for sexual fulfillment but not necessarily a need for affection.

2. Does your conversation with each other tend to be enjoyable for both of you? I describe characteristics of a good and bad conversation. Try practicing some of the good characteristics and avoid the bad ones.

3. Do you enjoy a conversation where you are being completely honest with each other? You probably do as long as your spouse avoids demands, disrespect, and anger. Why do you think I do not view these as legitimate aspects of honesty and openness? Chapter 12 addresses the issue of honesty in more detail.

4. In the past forty years I have seen a revolution in our thinking regarding financial support. Dual careers are now the norm instead of the exception. Has this revolution in thinking affected your need for financial support? In other words, do you still feel your husband should support you and the family? Or are you happy to support your husband if you can earn more than he does?

5. As far as I am concerned, the most important thing you can do for your children is to stay married. Divorce would definitely put them at a disadvantage in life. But what can you do for them beyond just staying married? That's where the need for family commitment comes in. Not only is a father's involvement in the training of the children good for the children, but it is one of the most important ways to deposit love units into his wife's Love Bank. Am I right? How

much pleasure do you feel when your husband is spending time with your children?

6. Does my "irresistible husband" sound attractive (to the wife) and realistic (to the husband)?

chapter seven

IDENTIFYING AND MEETING IMPORTANT EMOTIONAL NEEDS

When you and your spouse were married, you promised and expected to care for each other for the rest of your lives. And as I have already shown, you care for each other by meeting each other's most important emotional needs.

Of course, to fulfill your promise to each other, you must know which needs are most important. So let me help you identify those needs and show you how you can meet them for the rest of your lives.

What are your most important emotional needs? Only you can identify them. And your spouse is the only one who can identify his or her needs. Though I may know the emotional needs of the average person, I do not know the particular needs of any individual until that person tells me what they are.

It is difficult for most people to identify their needs without a little help, so in the last two chapters, I described some of the most common emotional needs. From that list of ten needs, you may have identified some of the needs that are most important to you. Now it's time for you to make a list of your selections.

The Emotional Needs Questionnaire

In appendix B, I have provided the Emotional Needs Questionnaire. Make two enlarged copies of this questionnaire so that both you and your spouse can complete it.

Remember, an emotional need is a craving that, when satisfied, makes you feel happy and fulfilled and, when unsatisfied, makes you feel unhappy and frustrated. Try to determine what gives you the most pleasure when you have it and what creates the most frustration when you don't have it. Put on your list needs you know you have that I did not include in the last two chapters, if there are any. Try to think of everything you crave in life, and if there is something that is very important to your happiness, include it on the list. But when you do, try to define it as clearly as you can so that your spouse will understand what it is.

One other point must be mentioned before you complete this questionnaire. When people have lost their love for their spouse, it's common for them to have important emotional needs that they may not want their spouse to meet. They may have been hurt and they do not want to lower their defenses enough to allow their spouse to meet important emotional needs that will make them vulnerable to more suffering. For now, I encourage you to identify your most important emotional needs even though you may not want your spouse to meet them at this time. That way you will know what you can do to make each other the happiest when you have learned to protect each other. (I will be discussing the topic of protection in part 3 of this book.)

After you have answered the questions of the Emotional Needs Questionnaire, there is a place on the last page for you to rank all of the needs according to their priority for you. Imagine for a moment that your spouse is willing and able to meet only one of the ten needs, and is unwilling or unable to meet any of the rest. If that were the case, which of the ten emotional needs would you select? Which emotional need, when met, would make you the happiest and, when unmet, would make you the most frustrated?

Before you answer, consider this: If you do not choose sexual fulfillment as the most important emotional need, you and your spouse may never have sex together. If you do not choose affection, your spouse may never hug or kiss you. If you do not choose financial support, your spouse may not earn a dime throughout your life together. Which need, when met, would have the best chance of causing you to be in love with your spouse? The need you select should be ranked number 1.

As you know, your marriage will probably not survive if only one of your needs is met. So if you were to choose one more need from the list, remembering that all the others would be unmet by your spouse, which would you choose? That should be ranked number 2. Continue ranking your needs in order of their importance to you until you have chosen five. Each time you choose one, remember to consider all the others to be lost causes.

The reason that I encourage you to select only five from the list is that I want you to become experts in meeting only the most important needs. You will waste your effort by meeting needs of lesser importance. Quite frankly, we cannot be experts at everything, so in marriage as in life itself, we must all set priorities if we are to achieve our objectives. And your objective of being in love with each other will require both you and your spouse to focus your attention on the other's most important needs.

> **Your objective of being in love with each other will require both you and your spouse to focus your attention on the other's most important needs.**

I'll repeat the point I made a little earlier. At this moment, you may not want your spouse to meet any of your emotional needs. Your Love Bank may have fallen to such a low point that you have no interest in your spouse doing anything for you, let alone meeting your most important emotional needs. If that's the case, try to remember what you needed most from your spouse before your marriage got so bad. I want you and your spouse to describe your important emotional needs to each other even if you don't want each other to meet them just yet.

Before you leave this assignment, give your list of five needs one last look and give special attention to those you did not include. If your spouse meets all five of the needs you have listed,

ACTION STEP

Complete the Emotional Needs Questionnaire

will you be happy? Will it trigger the feeling of love? If your spouse fails to meet a need that is not included on your list, will it threaten to ruin your marriage? If there is a sixth need that either of you feels must be included to ensure the success of your marriage, add it to the list. But then let the other spouse also add a sixth need to his or her list.

My experience with most couples is that if they do an outstanding job meeting each other's top two emotional needs, that's all it takes to create romantic love. If couples do a reasonably good job meeting the other three, they add insurance to their marriage. But couples who try to meet all ten needs try to do too much and usually do a poor or mediocre job on the needs that are most important. In those marriages, even though a great deal of effort is made, the results are very disappointing. But couples who focus attention on the needs that mean the most, and ignore the rest, have sensational marriages.

So the needs you and your spouse ranked number 1 and number 2 should get your very special attention. They are the ones you want to be experts in meeting for each other. If you leave them unmet in your marriage, your love for each other will be at risk. If someone outside your marriage meets them, he or she will become attractive enough to threaten your marriage. Affairs are usually caused when someone outside the marriage meets one of the two most important emotional needs.

Complete the Emotional Needs Questionnaire now, before you continue reading this chapter.

Agree to Meet Each Other's Needs

Now that you and your spouse have identified your five (or six) most important emotional needs, make a trade. Agree to meet your spouse's emotional needs in return for your spouse agreeing to meet yours.

When you first married, you promised to care for each other, but the details of that care were so vague that you have probably failed to live up to your promise. Now you have the details you should have had then. So let's go back to the day you married, now that you have a much clearer understanding of what it will take to make each other happy. I encourage you to make a new marital agreement, this time specifying the care you both need from each other.

I have provided this agreement for you in appendix C (Agreement to Meet the Most Important Emotional Needs). There are spaces in the agreement for you to name the emotional needs you have identified as most important to each of you. After completing the agreement, sign it as an expression of your commitment to meet those needs for each other.

ACTION STEP

Complete the Agreement to Meet the Most Important Emotional Needs

It would be wise to review your list every year because needs change over time. In some years, the change may not be very great—maybe just a slight reordering of needs. But in the year of your first child, if you have not had one yet, new needs are likely to replace some of the old ones. That's when you must remind yourselves that care means meeting each other's most important emotional needs, even when those needs change during your lifetime together. And to know what they are, you will need to check with each other regularly.

If you have been hurt so badly and your Love Bank balance is so low that you do not want your spouse to meet your most important emotional needs, postpone signing this agreement. Instead, read the next two sections of the book, which will show you how to protect each other and negotiate fairly. After you have learned these lessons, and feel less defensive, come back to this agreement, sign it, and read the rest of part 2.

Evaluate Your Effectiveness

You have already identified your most important emotional needs, and that's an essential first step. By agreeing with each other to become experts at meeting those needs, you have taken the second step. Now if you develop the habits that will make you the expert you agreed to be, you will provide each other with the care that you expect in your marriage.

Most people feel that they can meet their spouse's emotional needs if they simply know what they are. Affection, conversation, sexual fulfillment—these shouldn't be too difficult to manage. Besides, you used to do a good job meeting many of each other's emotional needs or you wouldn't have married. Maybe all you need is a reminder to get back on track.

When you did a good job meeting each other's emotional needs, you were in the habit of doing so. Now you may have lost those habits, and new habits that are ineffective in meeting each other's needs have taken their place. So you may have to restore those old habits, or perhaps create new habits to meet needs that had not been important to you until now. And unless you ask each other how effective you are at meeting these needs, you will not know if your efforts are actually doing the job.

> Unless you ask each other how effective you are at meeting these needs, you will not know if your efforts are actually doing the job.

Discussions about whether or not your efforts are effective at meeting each other's emotional needs must be handled very delicately. It's easy to be offended when you learn that your efforts are not having the desired effect. That's why many married couples avoid evaluating each other's effectiveness until the situation has deteriorated almost to a point of no return. And then, instead of making sensitive assessments of each other's behavior, they often just blast away at each other, making demands, showing disrespect, and becoming angry.

It will probably be very tough for either of you to admit that an important emotional need is not being met as it should be. For one thing, you may be trying to be as supportive and encouraging to each other as possible. You certainly don't want to indulge in criticism, and yet, if you are dissatisfied with the way your partner is meeting your need, it's important to reveal that fact. You need a simple yet sensitive way to communicate your satisfaction or dissatisfaction with the way your important needs are being met.

One way that you and your spouse can evaluate each other's effectiveness in meeting each emotional need is to answer the following questions.

1. Are you satisfied with the way I am meeting this need?
2. If your answer is no, how would you like me to meet this need? Think of specific habits that you would like me to learn.
3. Do I meet this need often enough?
4. If not, how often would you like me to meet this need?

ACTION STEP

Answer the four questions about the most important emotional needs on your list.

If you answer these questions for each other every once in a while, this feedback will help you determine if your skills are adequate or if they need improvement.

Improve Your Skills

Your spouse's evaluation of how well you are meeting his or her needs considers two aspects of care—quality and quantity.

Quality is the way you go about meeting a need. For example, in meeting the need for conversation, you must learn how to make the conversation enjoyable for both you and your spouse. You simply cannot meet a need unless the quality of your care meets your spouse's minimum standard. But at the same time, it must also be something you enjoy with your spouse.

> Quality is the way
> you go about
> meeting a need.
> Quantity is how
> often and how much
> time you spend
> meeting a need.

Quantity is how often and how much time you spend meeting a need. Some people don't require fulfillment very often, while others want it frequently. Conversation is one of those needs that, for some, may be satisfied with a short chat, and for others, may need more time.

When you learn to meet each other's emotional needs, you must satisfy both the quality and quantity requirements to make your spouse happy. Quantity is fairly easy to understand, because your spouse will tell you how often and how much he or she wants the need met.

ACTION STEP

Consult the additional resources for insight and motivation to meet each other's needs.

But quality is more difficult to communicate. Sometimes even the one with the need does not understand exactly what's missing. If you know that quality improvements are needed but you are at a loss as to how to make them, I suggest that you read *His Needs, Her Needs: Building an Affair-proof Marriage* and its accompanying workbook *Five Steps to Romantic Love.* The workbook contains the worksheets that I use in my practice to help couples become experts at meeting each other's emotional needs.

I have also produced an audio series, *His Needs, Her Needs: Habits for a Lifetime of Passion,* to help motivate you to create the habits that will meet each other's emotional needs. If you are having any problems knowing what to do or trouble motivating yourselves, I strongly encourage you to use this audio series.

Meet Each Other's Needs in Ways That Are Mutually Enjoyable

There are many ways to meet each other's emotional needs. Some of them will be enjoyable to the one trying to meet the need and some will be unpleasant. When we are in love, we are tempted to meet each other's needs at all costs, even if it requires considerable sacrifice. (I'll explain why this is the case in chapter 15, The Three States of Mind in Marriage.) But I strongly advise a husband and wife to avoid sacrificing their own pleasure to bring pleasure to the other spouse. You should meet each other's needs only in ways that are enjoyable for both of you. Never expect your spouse to suffer to make you happy and don't suffer to make your spouse happy.

There is a great deal of wisdom behind this recommendation. Think about it. If you and your spouse care for each other, neither of you should want the other to suffer. How much gratification can you have knowing that your spouse is unhappy in the way he or she is meeting your needs? In fact most emotional needs can be met only when your spouse enjoys meeting them for you.

Take conversation, for example. If your spouse is bored by a particular topic of conversation but knows that you like to talk for hours, how can you possibly be fulfilled with conversation on that topic, knowing that he or she is very uncomfortable? The same is true for recreational companionship. Is it much fun to engage in an activity with someone who would rather be somewhere else?

Sexual fulfillment is particularly sensitive to mutual enjoyment. If one spouse forces himself or herself into having sex as often as needed, does that make it fulfilling? I've counseled many wives who have agreed to have sex as often as requested, yet their husband leaves every experience fuming. Why? Because he knows she is only doing it for him, not because she desires sex. He is sexually fulfilled only if she enjoys making love too.

> **Never expect your spouse to suffer to make you happy and don't suffer to make your spouse happy.**

So the skills you learn that meet your spouse's emotional needs must take your own feelings into account. If you are to be a skilled conversationalist, you must select topics that interest you as much as they interest your spouse. Your recreational activities must be enjoyable for you as well as for him or her. And whenever you make love, the skills you develop must enable you to join your spouse in the sexual experience. Your sacrifice in the area of needs fulfillment will not be satisfying to your partner.

There's a second important reason to avoid sacrificing your own enjoyment when meeting your spouse's needs. You will not be meeting your spouse's need very often if you don't enjoy doing it. We tend to do what we enjoy the most and we avoid what we don't enjoy. The more you enjoy doing something, the more often you will want to do it. The less you enjoy doing something, the less you will want to do it. If your spouse wants you to meet his or her needs often, you must enjoy the experience.

A third reason for not sacrificing when meeting emotional needs is that it can create an aversive reaction. There are some spouses who are so disciplined that they can force themselves to sacrifice their feelings for an important cause. In marriage these people know that they are expected to meet certain needs but do not know how to enjoy meeting them. They were brought up to believe that many of life's responsibilities require sacrifice, so they suffer in their effort to meet their spouse's needs.

Sex is a good example of a need that these people try to meet by sacrificing their feelings. Whenever they make love, they suffer. But because they know it's required of them, they do it anyway. Eventually, after they have forced themselves to suffer for a while, they develop what psychologists call an aversion. It's a powerful negative emotional reaction that is conditioned to any unpleasant experience.

> **It's your mutual happiness that will make your marriage successful.**

When an aversion to sex is formed, every sex act creates emotional symptoms that are overwhelmingly unpleasant. Eventually the pain is so great that sex must be abandoned entirely, in spite of the person's strong belief that it must be performed at all costs.

While an aversion to sex or anything else can eventually be overcome by carefully undoing the learned association between the act and the emotional pain, it is far better never to create the aversive reaction in the first place. If you and your spouse learn to meet each other's needs in ways that take each other's feelings into account, you will never experience the pain of an aversive reaction.

Don't make the mistake of thinking that your marriage should be built on sacrifice. It's your mutual happiness that will make your marriage successful, and personal sacrifice, however well intentioned it is, will undermine mutual happiness. Neither of you wants the other to meet your needs reluctantly, and the only way to avoid that sad outcome is to learn to meet them in ways that you both enjoy.

If a husband suffers whenever he is with his wife, and the wife suffers whenever she is with him, how long will that last? And how can anyone view that as a happy marriage?

In the next chapter, I will introduce you to a rule that I encourage all couples to follow, but it's impossible to follow this rule if you both think that suffering is required to make each other happy. The only way to follow it is to be certain that you are both happy when you are meeting each other's emotional needs. Then the rule will be easy to follow.

Follow Through

Step 1: Complete the Emotional Needs Questionnaire.

Step 2: Sign the Agreement to Meet the Most Important Emotional Needs.

Step 3: Evaluate your effectiveness.

Step 4: Create plans to improve your skill.

Step 5: Learn to meet each other's needs in ways that are mutually enjoyable.

Additional Resources

Willard F. Harley, Jr. *His Needs, Her Needs: Building an Affair-proof Marriage.* Grand Rapids: Revell, 1986, 1994, 2001. The ten most important emotional needs of husbands and wives are described along with how those needs can be met in marriage.

Willard F. Harley, Jr. *Five Steps to Romantic Love.* Grand Rapids: Revell, 1993. This is a workbook to accompany *His Needs, Her Needs* that contains the worksheets that I use in my practice to help couples learn to become experts at meeting each other's emotional needs.

Willard F. Harley, Jr. *His Needs, Her Needs: Habits for a Lifetime of Passion.* St. Paul: Marriage Builders, 1999. This audio series helps motivate you to create the habits that will meet each other's emotional needs. When you order the audio series, the book *His Needs, Her Needs* and the workbook *Five Steps to Romantic Love* are included. To order this audio series, call Marriage Builders at 1-888-639-1639.

chapter eight

THE POLICY OF
UNDIVIDED
ATTENTION

Before you were married, you and your spouse probably spent the majority of your leisure time together. And the time you spent together was probably the most enjoyable part of every day. Spending time alone with each other was your highest priority, and you may even have canceled other plans when you had an opportunity to be together. You probably tried to talk to each other every day. If you couldn't physically be together, you talked on the telephone, sometimes for hours. And when you were together, you gave each other your **undivided attention.**

But after marriage, like so many other couples, you probably find that you can be in the same room together and yet ignore each other emotionally. What's even worse, you may find that you are not even in the same room very often, particularly after your children arrived.

One of the more difficult aspects of marriage counseling is scheduling time for it. Counselors must often work evenings and weekends because most couples will not give up work for their appointments. Then they must schedule around a host of evening and weekend activities that take a husband and wife in opposite directions.

But finding time for an appointment is easy compared to arranging time for the couple to be together to carry out their first assignment. Many couples think that a counselor will solve their problem with weekly conversations in his office. It doesn't occur to them that it's what they do after they leave the office that saves the marriage. To improve marriage, couples must schedule time together—time to give each other their undivided attention.

> **To improve marriage, couples must schedule time together—time to give each other their undivided attention.**

It's incredible how many couples have tried to talk me out of their spending more time together. They begin by trying to convince me that it's impossible. Then they go on to the argument that it's impractical. But in the end, they usually agree with me that without time for undivided attention, they cannot re-create the love they once had for each other.

And that's the point. Unless you and your spouse schedule time each week for undivided attention, it will be almost impossible to meet each other's most important emotional needs. That's because other less important objectives will crowd out the time that it takes to meet those needs.

You and your spouse have identified your most important emotional needs and you have agreed to meet them for each other. Now you must take a step that will make it all possible—you must clear space in your schedule for each other. You must make time to be together.

For most men romance is sex and recreation; for most women it's affection and conversation. When all four come together, men and women alike call it romance and they deposit the most love units possible in each other's Love Bank. That makes these categories somewhat inseparable whenever you spend time together. My advice is to try to combine them all, and in this chapter I will focus on meeting these four needs.

To help you achieve the essential but difficult objective of spending enough time together to meet each other's needs, I encourage you to follow the Policy of Undivided Attention.

THE POLICY OF UNDIVIDED ATTENTION

Give your spouse your undivided attention a minimum of fifteen hours each week, using the time to meet his or her need for affection, sexual fulfillment, conversation, and recreational companionship.

This policy will help you avoid one of the most common mistakes in marriage—neglecting each other's most important emotional needs. I will try to clarify this policy for you by offering three corollaries: privacy, objectives, and amount of time.

Corollary 1: Privacy

The time you plan to be together should not include children (who are awake), relatives, or friends. Establish privacy so that you are better able to give each other your undivided attention.

It is essential for you as a couple to spend time alone. When you have time alone, you have a much greater opportunity to meet each other's emotional needs and make Love Bank deposits. Without privacy, undivided attention is almost impossible, and without undivided attention, you are unable to meet the emotional needs of affection, conversation, and sexual fulfillment.

First, I recommend that you learn to be together without your children. I'm amazed at how difficult this is for couples, especially when the children are very young. Many couples don't think that children interfere with their privacy. To them, an evening with their children *is* privacy. And, technically, when they are with their children they are meeting at least one emotional need—the need for family commitment. The problem is that if they are never together without their children, they are not able to meet other needs that usually have a higher priority.

Learn to be together without your children.

Of course, they know they can't make love with children around. But I believe that the presence of children prevents much more than lovemaking. When children are present, they interfere with affection and intimate conversation that are crucial needs in marriage. Besides, affection and intimate conversation usually lead to lovemaking, and without them, you will find that your lovemaking suffers. And if your recreational companionship always includes your children, you will be so restricted in what you find mutually enjoyable that you will be tempted to make one of the biggest mistakes in marriage—spending your most enjoyable leisure time apart from each other.

Second, I recommend that friends and relatives not be present during your time together. This may mean that after everything has been scheduled, there is little time left for friends and relatives. If that's the case, you're too busy, but at least you will not be sacrificing your love for each other to have time with friends and relatives.

Undivided Attention

Time spent alone with your spouse during which you pay close attention to each other.

Now you must understand what giving undivided attention means. It's what you did when you were dating. You probably would not have married if you had ignored each other on dates. You may have parked your car somewhere just to be completely alone and to rid yourselves of all distractions. That's the quality of undivided attention I'm encouraging you to create.

When you see a movie together, the time you are watching it would not usually count toward your time for undivided attention, unless you behave like the couple who sat in front of my wife and me last week. It's the same with television and sporting events. Though it is good to participate together in these activities, they do not fulfill the requirement for giving undivided attention to each other.

Friends and relatives should not be present during your time together.

Now if you schedule time to be alone with each other, what should you do with this time? The second corollary answers that question.

Corollary 2: Objectives

During the time you are together, create activities that will meet the emotional needs of affection, sexual fulfillment, conversation, and recreational companionship.

After marriage, women often try to get their husband to meet their emotional needs for conversation and affection, without meeting their husband's needs for sexual and recreational companionship. Men, on the other hand, want their wife to meet their needs for sexual fulfillment and recreational companionship, without meeting her needs for affection and conversation. Neither strategy works very well. Women often resent having sex without affection and conversation first, and men resent talking and being affectionate with no hope for sex or recreation. By combining the fulfillment of all four needs into a single event, however, both spouses have their needs met and enjoy the entire time together.

A man should never assume that just because he is in bed with his wife, sex is there for the taking. In many marriages, that mistake creates resentment and confusion. Most men eventually learn that if they spend the evening giving their wife their undivided attention, with conversation and affection, sex becomes a very natural and mutually enjoyable way to end the evening.

But there are some women who don't see the connection either. They want their husbands to give them the most attention when there is no possibility for sex. In fact knowing that affection and intimate conversation often lead a man to wanting sex, they try to be affectionate when they are out in a crowd. That tactic can lead to just as much resentment in a man as nightly sexual "ambushes" create in a woman. Take my word for it, the four needs of affection, conversation, recreational companionship, and sexual fulfillment are best met when they are met together.

Since you are in the process of learning how to meet each other's emotional needs and overcome habits that hurt each other, I suggest that you use part of your fifteen hours together to achieve these important objectives. I also suggest that you put a special effort into learning how to meet the needs of affection, conversation, sexual fulfillment, and recreational companionship. That way you will be able to make the most of your fifteen hours together each week.

> **The four needs of affection, conversation, recreational companionship, and sexual fulfillment are best met when they are met together.**

Your time for undivided attention should be the best time of the week for both of you. But it may not begin that way. If you do not yet know how to meet each other's emotional needs, you may find your time together boring or even unpleasant. This is particularly true if your conversation includes demands, disrespect, and angry outbursts. As I mentioned earlier, if you want to meet the need for conversation, you must learn to avoid hurting each other with what you say. (I will explain how to do that in part 3 of this book.)

But if you do not schedule this time to be together now, you will never have the opportunity to learn how to make it enjoyable for both of you and how to avoid making it unpleasant. When you have finally learned to meet each other's needs and avoid hurting each other, the time that you schedule for each other will become the best time of the week.

Don't waste precious weeks, months, and years hoping that somehow your relationship will improve. Take the first step toward ensuring your success by actually scheduling time for each other. And during your time together, do whatever it takes to make it the best fifteen hours of your week.

Corollary 3: Amount of Time

The number of hours you schedule to be together each week for undivided attention should reflect the quality of your marriage. If your marriage is satisfying to you and your spouse, schedule fifteen hours each week to be together. But if you suffer marital dissatisfaction, plan more time until marital satisfaction is achieved.

How much time do you need to sustain the feeling of love for each other? Believe it or not, there really is an answer to this question and it depends on the health of a marriage. If a couple is deeply in love with each other and finds that their marital needs are being met, I have discovered that about fifteen hours each week of undivided attention is usually enough to sustain their love, as long as they use the time to meet each other's emotional needs. When a marriage is this healthy, either it's a new marriage or the couple has already been spending that amount of time with each other throughout their marriage. Without fifteen hours of undivided attention each week, a couple simply can't do what it takes to sustain their feeling of love for each other.

When I apply the fifteen-hour principle to marriages, I usually recommend that the time be evenly distributed throughout the week, two to three hours each day. When time is bunched up—all hours only on the weekend—good results are not as predictable. Spouses need to be emotionally reconnected almost on a daily basis to meet each other's most important emotional needs.

> Spouses need to be emotionally reconnected almost on a daily basis to meet each other's most important emotional needs.

The reason I have so much difficulty getting couples to spend time with each other is that when I first see them for counseling, they have forgotten how to have a good time with each other. Their relationship does not do anything for them, and the time spent with each other seems like a total waste at first. But if I can motivate them to schedule the time together every week, they learn to re-create the romantic experiences that first nurtured their love relationship. Without scheduling that time, they have little hope of restoring the love they once had for each other.

Fifteen hours a week is often not enough time to jump-start a relationship if the couple is not in love with each other. In this case I usually suggest increasing the number of hours spent alone together so that they can learn more quickly the skills that will meet each other's emotional needs. I sometimes suggest abandoning most other responsibilities so that they can spend twenty-five or thirty hours a week of undivided attention until they can meet each other's emotional needs almost effortlessly. By the time that happens, they are both in love with each other again. In some cases I have even recommended a two-to-three-week vacation together so they can give each other undivided attention around the clock.

Your time together is too important to the security of your marriage to neglect. It's more important than time spent doing anything else during the week, including time with your children and your job. Remember that the fifteen hours you should set aside is only equivalent to a part-time job. It isn't time you don't have; it's time you will use for something much less important if you don't use it for each other.

How can a workaholic businessman find time to have an affair? The man who couldn't be home for dinner because of his busy schedule is suddenly able to fit in a midafternoon rendezvous three times a week! How does he get his work done? The answer, of course, is that he had the time all along. It's simply a matter of priorities. He could just as easily have spent the time with his wife. Then they would have been in love with each other. Instead, he's in love with someone else, all because he thought his work was more important than his relationship with his wife.

Your time together is too important to the security of your marriage to neglect.

If you have not been in the habit of spending fifteen hours a week for undivided attention with your spouse, it will mean that something else that takes fifteen hours will have to go. But you have about 110 total waking hours each week that you spend doing something, and if you schedule your time productively, you will find that the fifteen hours you lose will have been spent on your least important goals. And you will put in its place fifteen hours for your most important goal. Think of it—your highest priority will take the place of your lowest priority. It will radically change your life for the better, because in exchange for something that really isn't that important to you, you will be investing in the single most important part of your life—your relationship with your spouse.

Learning to Set Aside Time for Undivided Attention

It should be obvious to you that it will take time to meet most of each other's emotional needs. Unless you schedule that time, you simply won't get the job done. Time has a way of slipping away if you don't set it aside for important objectives. And what objective is more important than you and your spouse being in love with each other?

To help you plan your week with each other's emotional needs in mind, I encourage you to meet with your spouse at 3:30 Sunday afternoon to look over each other's schedule for the coming week. That's the time for you to be sure that you have provided for each other. And while you're at it, try to plan a little extra time just in case an emergency arises that prevents you from being together the full fifteen hours you originally plan.

In appendix D you will find a worksheet to help you plan your time together and keep a record of how the time was spent. The Time for Undivided Attention Worksheet introduces topics that you both should consider when planning your time and later evaluating it.

The "Planned Time Together" part of this worksheet should be completed when you first schedule your fifteen hours. Then, the "Actual Time Together" should be completed throughout the week after each date is completed. On the following Sunday afternoon, when you are scheduling time for the next week, you should evaluate how the last week actually turned out.

Another form, the Time for Undivided Attention Graph, in appendix E, provides a record of how many hours you actually spend each week giving each other your undivided attention. I encourage you to put this graph in a prominent place in your home, like on the refrigerator door, so that your children can see if you are achieving your goal. It will help them understand why you cannot be with them part of each week, and it will also teach them what they will need to do some day to keep love in their own marriages.

Neglect of emotional needs not only withdraws love units, it also turns out to be the single most important reason that women divorce men, and they divorce men twice as often as men divorce women. If you want to keep your wife around, men, listen up. She needs your undivided attention, and if you don't give it to her at least fifteen hours a week, not only will you lose her love, you risk losing her.

You and your spouse fell in love with each other because you met some of each other's most important emotional needs, and

> **ACTION STEP**
>
> At 3:30 on Sunday afternoon, schedule fifteen hours for undivided attention, indicating on the Time for Undivided Attention Worksheet when you will be together and what you will be doing.

> **Neglect of emotional needs not only withdraws love units, it also turns out to be the single most important reason that women divorce men.**

At 3:30 on the following Sunday afternoon, use the Time for Undivided Attention Graph to review your schedule, see how you did, and plan for the next week.

the only way to stay in love is to keep meeting those needs. Even when the feeling of love begins to fade, or when it's gone entirely, it's not necessarily gone for good. It can be recovered whenever you both go back to being experts at making Love Bank deposits.

Meeting important emotional needs is only half of the story, however. While that's how couples make the most Love Bank deposits, they must be sure that they're not depositing into a sieve. They must also avoid making Love Bank *withdrawals.*

The next section introduces several concepts that will help couples avoid hurting each other. You'd think that causing pain and suffering would be the last thing a married couple would want to do to each other, and yet it's done instinctively and habitually all the time. Unless you protect each other from your destructive habits and instincts, you will hurt each other so much that eventually your Love Bank accounts will be in the red—you will hate each other.

You have already read quite a bit in this section on making Love Bank deposits, and you may feel as if you have learned enough to put your marriage back on track. But don't stop reading now. This next section is in some ways more important than the one you've just read, because if you don't know how to protect each other, you may destroy opportunities to care for each other. The two go hand in hand—without protection, care is not possible. So please read on.

Follow Through

Step 1: Copy and enlarge the Time for Undivided Attention Worksheet (appendix D) and the Time for Undivided Attention Graph (appendix E).

Step 2: At 3:30 on Sunday afternoon, schedule fifteen hours for undivided attention, indicating on the Time for Undivided Attention Worksheet when you will be together and what you will be doing. Remind each other that this is to be the best time of the week for both of you—a time that you will be trying to make each other the happiest.

Step 3: Spend time together as you planned it, documenting how much time and how it was spent on the Time for Undivided Attention Worksheet.

Step 4: At 3:30 on the following Sunday afternoon, review the past week's Time for Undivided Attention Worksheet, and prepare a new one for the coming week. Copy the total time you spent together on your Time for Undivided Attention Graph.

Step 5: Continue to plan your time for undivided attention each Sunday afternoon for the rest of your lives. You can eliminate the worksheet and graph when you are in the habit of meeting each other's most important emotional needs during your time together.

part three

HOW TO AVOID LOVE BANK WITHDRAWALS

chapter nine

LEARNING TO
PROTECT
EACH OTHER

The love you and your spouse have for each other is directly affected by almost all of your habits. Whenever you do something, you are either depositing love units in your spouse's Love Bank or withdrawing them.

In the part of this book you just read, I explained how you could learn habits that would deposit the most love units possible. But Love Bank deposits will not do your marriage much good if other habits lead to Love Bank withdrawals. Caring for your spouse by meeting his or her emotional needs is not enough to maintain the feeling of love. You must also protect your spouse from habits that cause his or her unhappiness.

Neither you nor your spouse married to hurt each other. Yet, if you are not careful, you can become the greatest source of each other's unhappiness. And if you don't make a special effort to protect each other from your own selfish instincts and habits, it's inevitable.

I'm sure you tried to protect each other's feelings during courtship. Quite frankly, if you had not tried to be thoughtful then, you probably would not have married each other. Inconsiderate behavior withdraws so many love units that couples who indulge in such behavior don't usually date very long, let alone marry, because it destroys the love they have for each other. Meet-

> **Meeting important emotional needs creates the feeling of love, but thoughtfulness keeps it alive.**

ing important emotional needs creates the feeling of love, but thoughtfulness keeps it alive.

Since your wedding day, your thoughtfulness may have slipped a peg or two. The pressures of life you face may have convinced you that you cannot always worry about how your spouse feels, and you may have found yourself willing to sacrifice your spouse's feelings to get what you want. It's likely that you fight with your spouse whenever you don't see eye to eye, instead of trying to solve problems in ways that work well for both of you.

If you have noticed that you and your spouse have become increasingly thoughtless to each other over the years, your marriage has been invaded by Love Busters.

What Are Love Busters?

Whenever you do something that makes your spouse unhappy, you withdraw some love units. A single careless act is bad enough, but if you repeatedly do something that makes him or her unhappy, your Love Bank withdrawals can become serious enough to threaten your spouse's love for you. I call habits that cause repeated withdrawals **Love Busters,** because that's what they do—they destroy the feeling of love.

> **Love Busters**
>
> Repeated behavior of one spouse that makes the other spouse unhappy.

In the simplest terms, Love Busters are those things you do on a regular basis that make your spouse unhappy. They rob enough love units from your account in your spouse's Love Bank to destroy romantic love. As I already mentioned, almost everything you do will make either Love Bank deposits or Love Bank withdrawals. And, sadly, in marriage you are far more likely to make withdrawals than deposits because there are so many more ways to make them.

Lack of empathy is at the core of the problem. Once, while watching a *Star Trek* episode, I was struck with what we are all up against. Dr. Spock had volunteered to be possessed by an alien presence so that it could communicate with Captain Kirk of the Starship Enterprise. As soon as it entered Dr. Spock's body, its first reaction was, "Oh, how lonely you must all feel."

You can become the greatest source of each other's unhappiness.

You see, in the alien world, they were all connected to each other through mental telepathy so that each one could feel what everyone else felt. They were all emotionally bonded to each other. But as soon as the alien possessed Spock's body, it realized that we humans are all emotionally cut off from each other. And it viewed our state as incredibly isolated and lonely.

One of the most important consequences of our emotional isolation is that we cannot feel the way we affect others. This creates the temptation to do something that pleases us even when it hurts others, because we don't feel the pain we cause. If we were emotionally connected to others as the aliens were, we would be far less tempted to do anything thoughtless—gaining at someone else's expense—because in doing so, we would be hurting ourselves as well.

And that's what I always seem to be battling when I try to encourage one spouse to avoid doing anything that would hurt the other spouse. I can't seem to inspire empathy. Each spouse complains about how thoughtless the other spouse is, without much awareness of his or her own thoughtlessness. For example, you may find your spouse's habit of ignoring you when you come home from work extremely annoying. But how often do you

Lack of empathy helps make thoughtlessness possible.

stop to consider your own annoying habit of coming home late from work without so much as a phone call?

Lack of empathy helps make thoughtlessness possible. Since we don't feel what others feel, we tend to minimize the negative effect we have on them and consider our thoughtlessness benign. You may regard an angry outburst as a way of expressing your deepest emotions; disrespect is just helping your spouse gain proper perspective; and a demand is nothing more than encouraging your spouse to do what he or she should have done all along. You don't see any of these as gaining at your spouse's expense, because you don't feel the pain you inflict. But whenever you are the cause of your spouse's unhappiness, one thing's for sure—Love Bank withdrawals are taking place.

> **Five Categories of Love Busters**
>
> Selfish demands, disrespectful judgments, angry outbursts, annoying behavior, and dishonesty.

In marriage there are a host of Love Busters—ways that spouses make each other unhappy. But I've found that the most common Love Busters in marriage fall into only five categories: selfish demands, disrespectful judgments, angry outbursts, annoying behavior, and dishonesty.

The first three of these Love Busters are instinctive, yet thoughtless, ways to try to get what you want from each other. When a request doesn't work, a spouse will often revert to a demand ("I don't care how you feel—do it or else!"). If that doesn't get the job done, a spouse will try disrespectful judgments ("If you had any sense and were not so lazy and selfish, you would do it"). And then, when all of that fails, an angry outburst often represents the last-ditch effort ("I'll see to it that you regret not having done it").

> Causing your spouse's unhappiness withdraws love units from his or her Love Bank.

Of course, in the long run, demands, disrespect, and anger don't really get you what you want. If you are demanding, disrespectful, and angry, your spouse tends to be less caring and considerate of you and will actually do *less* for you. Instead of getting you what you need, demands, disrespect, and anger cause your spouse to resist.

But when you indulge in these three Love Busters, you do more than fail to get what you need. You also destroy the love your spouse has for you. All of these habits cause your spouse to be unhappy. And that causes Love Bank withdrawals.

The fourth Love Buster, annoying behavior, includes habits and activities that may make you happy but drive your spouse nuts. Marriage is a partnership of incredibly close quarters, where just about anything you or your spouse does is almost sure to affect the other. If you want to stay in love with each other, your habits and activities should make Love Bank deposits, not withdrawals.

Finally, the fifth Love Buster, dishonesty, causes massive Love Bank withdrawals whenever it's discovered. And spouses will usually discover each other's dishonesty, because of their emotional closeness to each other. If you or your spouse has a tendency to lie or distort the truth, chase that bad habit out of your marriage before it ruins everything.

The Parable of the Net

Marriage is like a fishing net. Each day fishermen use their nets to catch fish and sell them at the market. One fisherman takes his fish from the net every day but lets debris from the ocean accumulate there. Eventually so much debris is caught in the net that he can hardly cast it out of the boat, and when he does, it's almost impossible to retrieve. Finally, in a fit of anger, he cuts the net loose and goes home without it. He's unable to catch and sell fish again until he buys another net.

Another fisherman removes debris every time he retrieves the net with the fish he caught. Each time he casts his net, it's clean and ready to catch more fish. As a result, he catches and sells enough fish to support himself and his family.

In this parable, the fish are emotional needs met in marriage and the debris is Love Busters, habits that cause unhappiness. Bad marriages are like the first fisherman's net. Angry outbursts, disrespectful judgments, annoying behavior, selfish demands, and dishonesty accumulate over time. The burden of the unhappiness they cause ruins a couple's willingness and ability to meet each other's emotional needs. Eventually the marriage provides no benefits to either spouse and ends in divorce or emotional separation.

Good marriages are like the second fisherman's net. Love Busters are eliminated as soon as they appear, making it easy for each spouse to meet the other's emotional needs.

I would like to show you how to keep debris from your net. You and your spouse can do that by identifying the Love Busters that destroy your love for each other and then learning habits that override their destructive influences. In the next two chapters I will describe Love Busters in more detail, help you identify those that are causing your marriage the greatest harm, and show you how to pick them out of your net so that you can harvest a netfull of love units.

Key Principles

- If you don't make a special effort to protect each other from your own selfish instincts and habits, you can become the greatest source of each other's unhappiness.

- Lack of empathy helps make thoughtlessness possible.

- A Love Buster is the repeated behavior of one spouse that makes the other spouse unhappy.

- The five categories of Love Busters are selfish demands, disrespectful judgments, angry outbursts, annoying behavior, and dishonesty.

Thinking It Through

1. In the beginning of this chapter, I made the following point: "Neither you nor your spouse married to hurt each other. Yet, if you are not careful, you can become the greatest source of each other's unhappiness." Does this statement apply to your marriage? Have you become each other's greatest source of unhappiness?

2. Discuss my *Star Trek* illustration. Does lack of empathy keep you and your spouse from protecting each other? If you were to feel each other's pain whenever you did something to hurt the other, how might it change your behavior?

3. The parable of the net describes two marriages. Which of them best describes your marriage? What kind of "debris" may remain in your net? What kind of "fish" are you failing to catch because of the debris?

chapter ten

LOVE
BUSTERS

As a psychologist, I have been fascinated by human instincts and habits. And I have been impressed by the difficulty most people have overriding them when they know beyond any doubt that they are self-defeating. For example, whenever I try to help an alcoholic learn to become sober, I'm amazed at how difficult it is, despite the person's recognition that alcohol causes him or her untold sorrow and suffering. It's like trying to train a moth to stay away from a lightbulb that will kill it if it gets too close.

Teaching married couples to stay away from the instincts and habits of demands, disrespect, and anger is just as difficult. And it's actually made much more difficult by the fact that few spouses see the danger of these behaviors. Many view these Love Busters as the way spouses should go about resolving their conflicts. In fact there are many well-respected counselors who argue that without these aids to communication, divorce is almost a certainty.

In this chapter I will do my best to convince you that demands, disrespect, and anger are to marriage what a lightbulb is to a moth. They are alluring but destructive. All three are inborn strategies to help you get what you want from your spouse, but they don't work. Rather, they make things worse and cause you to risk losing love for each other.

Of course, avoiding conflicts altogether doesn't work either. So as you avoid these Love Busters, you must substitute effective alternatives to problem solving. As I describe each of these Love Busters, I will also suggest habits that will be effective in problem solving, giving you what you need from each other.

Selfish Demands

We were all born with instincts to help us survive the trials and travails of life. Some instincts are very helpful and others are downright stupid and abusive. One of our more stupid and abusive instincts, especially in marriage, is making demands. If we make a request for something we want or need, and the request is turned down, our instincts encourage us to take more forceful steps. And the first thing that comes to mind is usually a demand.

> **Selfish Demands**
>
> Commanding your spouse to do things that would benefit you at your spouse's expense, with implied threat of punishment if refused.

Demands carry a threat of punishment—an if-you-refuse-me-you'll-regret-it kind of thing. In other words, you may dislike doing what I want, but if you don't do it, I'll see to it that you suffer even greater pain.

People who make demands don't seem to care how others feel. They think only of their own needs. "If you find it unpleasant to do what I want, tough! And if you refuse, I'll make it even tougher," is what they seem to be saying.

Demands depend on power. They don't work unless the demanding one has the power to make good on his or her threats. But who has power in marriage? Ideally, there is shared power, the husband and wife working together to accomplish mutual objectives. But when one spouse starts making demands—along with threats that are at least implied—it's a power play. The threatened spouse often strikes back, fighting fire with fire, power with power. Suddenly, it's a test of power—who will win the battle?

If the demanding partner doesn't have enough power to follow through on the threat, he or she often receives punishment, at least in the form of ridicule. But if power is fairly equal between a husband and wife, a battle rages until one or the other surrenders. In the end, the one meeting the demand feels deep resentment and is less likely to meet the need in the future. When the demand is not met, both spouses feel resentment.

You and your spouse must get from each other what you need most in your marriage. You must meet each other's emotional needs and be there for each other when you need help. But let me assure you that demands will not get the job done.

When I ask my wife, Joyce, to do something for me, she may cheerfully agree to it—or she may express her reluctance. This reluctance may be due to any number of things—her needs, her comfort level, or her sense of what's wise or fair. If I push my request, making it a demand, what am I doing? I am trying to override her reluctance. I am declaring that my wishes are more important than her feelings. And I'm threatening to cause her some distress if she doesn't do what I want.

Demands depend on power.

She now must choose one of two evils—my "punishment" on the one hand or whatever made her reluctant on the other. She may ultimately agree to my demand but she won't be happy about it. I may get my way but I'm gaining at her expense. My gain is her loss. And she will most certainly feel used.

"But you don't know my husband!" some wife may say. "He lies around the house all night and I can't get him to do a thing. The only time he lifts a finger is to press the remote control. If I don't demand that he get up and help me, nothing will get done."

"You can't be talking about my wife," a husband may say. "She only thinks about herself! She spends her whole life shopping and going out with her friends. If I didn't demand that she stay at home once in a while, I'd never see her."

Without a doubt, you and your spouse need to find effective ways to motivate each other to meet your needs. But demands are nothing short of abuse. In fact it's usually the first stage of verbal abuse that ultimately leads to fights in marriage.

If you make demands of your spouse and expect obedience, you are being controlling and manipulative. Your spouse will try to escape your abuse and, instead of becoming responsive to your needs, he or she will have as little to do with you as possible. Is that what you want? Do you want to drive your spouse away from you?

Neither you nor your spouse is a sergeant and neither of you is a private. You do not have the right to tell each other what to do and, if you try, you will find that it doesn't work. If you try to force your spouse to meet your needs, it becomes a temporary solution at best, and resentment is sure to rear its ugly head. Demands and other forms of manipulation do not build compatibility; they build resentment.

> **Demands are nothing short of abuse. Thoughtful requests are a wise alternative to selfish demands.**

There is a wise alternative to selfish demands, and that's thoughtful requests. This approach to getting what you need from each other begins by simply explaining what you would like and then asking your spouse how he or she would feel fulfilling your request. If he or she indicates that the request will be unpleasant to fulfill, discuss alternative, pleasant ways your spouse could help you.

"I've already tried that, and it doesn't work" may be your immediate reaction. It may be that your spouse simply indicates that whatever it is you want isn't something he or she wants to do. But that's where negotiation should begin. If you become a skilled negotiator, you will accept a negative reaction and try to figure out a way for your spouse to help enthusiastically with whatever it is you want.

> **Thoughtful Request**
>
> Respectfully explaining to your spouse what you would like and allowing your spouse the option of granting or denying your request.

In part 4 of this book, I'll explain how you can learn to negotiate successfully with each other. But remember, if you or your spouse is using the stupid and abusive instinct of selfish demands to try to get what you need, you will most certainly destroy the love you have for each other—and in the long run, you will not get what you need.

Disrespectful Judgments

When requests don't get you what you want, and demands don't work either, our instincts and habits often provide us with another stupid and abusive strategy—disrespectful judgments. Without a doubt, demands are abusive, but disrespectful judgments often make demands seem merciful in comparison.

In marriage spouses often use disrespectful judgments as clever disguises for demanding what they want. They present the problem as if it were really their spouse's personal shortcoming. They try to "straighten out" their spouse in an effort to get their way.

When we use disrespectful judgments, we rationalize our behavior by convincing ourselves that we're doing our spouse a big favor, to lift him or her from the darkness of confusion into the light of our superior perspective. If our spouse would only follow our advice, we tell ourselves, he or she could avoid many of life's pitfalls—and we would also get what we want.

A disrespectful judgment occurs whenever one spouse tries to impose a system of values and beliefs on the other. When a husband tries to force his point of view on his wife, he's just asking for trouble. When a wife assumes that her own views are right and her husband is woefully misguided—and tells him so—she enters a minefield.

In most cases a disrespectful judgment is simply a sophisticated way of getting what one spouse wants from the other. But

> **Disrespectful Judgment**
>
> Attempting to "straighten out" your spouse's attitudes, beliefs, and behavior by trying to impose on him or her your way of thinking through lecture, ridicule, threats, or other forceful means.

even when there is absolutely nothing in it for the disrespectful spouse, it's still a stupid and abusive strategy. It's stupid because it doesn't work, and it's abusive because it causes unhappiness. If we think we have the right—even the responsibility—to impose our view on our spouse, our efforts will almost invariably be interpreted as personally threatening, arrogant, rude, and incredibly disrespectful. That's when we make sizable withdrawals from the Love Bank.

How can you know if you're a perpetrator of disrespectful judgments? The simplest way to find out is to ask your spouse. But you may be a little confused as to what exactly you should ask. The Disrespectful Judgments Questionnaire will help you ask the right questions.

Disrespectful Judgments Questionnaire

Circle the number that best represents your feelings about the way your spouse tries to influence your attitudes, beliefs, and behavior. If you circle a number greater than 1 for any question, try to think of an example that you can share with your spouse and write it on a sheet of paper.

1. Does your spouse ever try to "straighten you out"?

Almost never		Sometimes		Much of the time	
1	2	3	4	5	6	7

2. Does your spouse ever lecture you instead of respectfully discussing issues?

Almost never		Sometimes		Much of the time	
1	2	3	4	5	6	7

3. Does your spouse seem to feel that his or her opinion is superior to yours?

Almost never		Sometimes		Much of the time	
1	2	3	4	5	6	7

4. When you and your spouse discuss an issue, does he or she interrupt you or talk so much that you are prevented from having a chance to explain your position?

Almost never		Sometimes		Much of the time	
1	2	3	4	5	6	7

5. Are you afraid to discuss your points of view with your spouse?

Almost never		Sometimes		Much of the time	
1	2	3	4	5	6	7

6. Does your spouse ever ridicule your point of view?

Almost never		Sometimes		Much of the time	
1	2	3	4	5	6	7

The scoring for this questionnaire is simple. Unless all of your spouse's answers are 1, you're probably engaging in disrespectful judgments. Almost all of us are guilty of this Love Buster from time to time, so don't be alarmed if you get some 2s or 3s. But if your spouse gave you any 4s, 5s, 6s, or 7s, you're at risk of losing your spouse's love for you because your disrespectful judgments are rising to the level of abuse.

If your spouse identifies you as one who makes disrespectful judgments, you may be tempted to make yet another disrespectful judgment and claim that he or she is wrong! Resist that temptation at all costs because in every case of abuse, the victim is a far better judge of the existence of abuse than the perpetrator. Take his or her word for it, and start working on a plan to eliminate whatever it is your spouse interprets as disrespect.

> **When we try to impose our opinions on our spouse, we imply that he or she has poor judgment.**

When we try to impose our opinions on our spouse, we imply that he or she has poor judgment. That's disrespectful. We may not say this in so many words, but it's the clear message that our spouse hears. If we valued his or her judgment more, we might question our own opinions. What if our spouse is right, and we're wrong?

I'm not saying that you can't disagree with your spouse. But you must respectfully disagree. Try to understand your spouse's reasoning. Present the information that brought you to your opinion and listen to the information your spouse brings. Entertain the possibility of changing your mind, instead of just pointing out how wrong your spouse is.

That's how respectful persuasion works. You see, each spouse brings two things into your marriage—wisdom and foolishness. Your marriage will thrive when you blend your value systems, with each one's wisdom overriding the other's foolishness. By sharing your ideas and sorting through the pros and cons, you can create a belief system superior to what either of you had alone. But unless you approach the task with mutual respect, the process won't work and you will destroy your love for each other in the process.

> **Respectful Persuasion**
> Presenting your reasoning behind your opinion and listening to your spouse's reasoning, with a willingness to admit that your spouse may be correct.

In most cases, disrespectful judgments are nothing more than stupid and abusive attempts to get what you want in your marriage.

As is the case with demands, disrespect doesn't work—it's simply a form of verbal abuse.

Angry Outbursts

When requests don't get what you want from your spouse, demands don't produce results, and disrespect doesn't work either, your instinct has one more stupid and abusive strategy up its sleeve—angry outbursts.

I view demands and disrespect as a ramping up to anger. Taken together, they define the typical fight of most couples. All three illustrate abuse in marriage, and what a tragedy it is. Instead of protecting each other, spouses become the greatest source of each other's unhappiness—and it's all instinctive. What I mean by that is that if you don't do something to stop it from happening, you will most certainly become the victim of each other's abusive instincts.

Instincts often help habits develop. An angry outburst is a good example of this. I've seen what looks like an angry outburst in a child at the moment of birth, and we can be assured that there wasn't much learning that caused that behavior. As a child grows, the way anger is expressed becomes increasingly sophisticated. But it isn't the instinct that's becoming sophisticated—it's the developing habit of an angry outburst, supported by the instinct, that makes it sophisticated.

> **Angry Outburst**
>
> Deliberately attempting to hurt your spouse because of anger, usually in the form of verbal or physical attack.

In marriage one of our most destructive behaviors is an angry outburst, when we intentionally try to hurt our spouse and cause massive Love Bank withdrawals. But it's something we do naturally—it's a habit that is developed by an instinct.

Although the primary reason for angry outbursts is trying to get what we want, our instinct makes us believe otherwise. It turns the situation into an issue of injustice. When we are angry, we usually feel that someone is deliberately making us unhappy (by not giving us what we want), which just isn't fair. In our angry state, we are convinced that reasoning won't work, and the

106

offender will keep upsetting us until he or she is taught a lesson. The only thing such people understand is punishment, we assume. Then they'll think twice about making us unhappy again!

We think we are using anger to protect ourselves, because it offers a simple solution to our problem—destroy the troublemaker. If our spouse turns out to be the troublemaker, we find ourselves hurting the one we've promised to cherish and protect. But when we're angry, we don't care about our spouse's feelings and we are willing to scorch the culprit if doing so will keep us from being hurt again.

When you become angry with your spouse, you threaten your spouse's safety and security—you fail to provide protection. Your spouse rises to the challenge and tries to destroy you in retaliation. In the end, you gain nothing from anger. Punishment does not solve marital problems; it only makes your punished spouse want to inflict punishment on you or, if that doesn't work, leave you. When anger wins, love loses.

> **When you become angry with your spouse, you threaten your spouse's safety and security— you fail to provide protection.**

Each of us has an arsenal of weapons we use when we're angry. If we think someone deserves to be punished, we unlock the gate and select an appropriate weapon. Sometimes the weapons are verbal (ridicule and sarcasm), sometimes they're devious plots to cause suffering, and sometimes they're physical. But they all have one thing in common: They are designed to hurt people. Since our spouse is at such close range, we can use our weapons to hurt him or her the most.

Some of the husbands and wives I've counseled have fairly harmless arsenals, maybe just a few awkward efforts at ridicule. Others are armed to nuclear proportions; their spouse's very life is in danger. The more dangerous your weapons are, the more important it is to control your temper. If you've ever lost your temper in a way that has caused your spouse great pain and suffering, you know you cannot afford to lose your temper again. You must go to extreme lengths to protect your spouse from yourself.

We can't change our instincts, but we can short-circuit their approach to solving a problem. If my instinct is to have angry outbursts, it doesn't mean that I must go around losing my temper. I can create new habits that keep my anger instinct in check. Habits that override inappropriate instincts are usually more difficult to create than habits that are not instinct driven, but it can be done. And in marriage, it must be done if you want to fall in love and stay in love.

Most effective anger management training programs focus attention on the creation of short-circuiting habits. Whenever a person begins to feel angry, he or she practices a behavior that has been shown to prevent an outburst. In the beginning, the new behavior is a conscious choice, something that is done regardless of how it feels to do it. Walking away from a frustrating situation is one example of a behavior that can short-circuit an angry outburst. Another is to follow a routine that relaxes your muscles and lowers adrenaline in your system. Eventually, with practice, the behavior that has proved effective in short-circuiting an angry outburst becomes a habit. Whenever the person begins to feel angry, the habit kicks in and the angry outburst is overcome.

> We can't change our instincts, but we can short-circuit their approach to solving a problem.

My approach to anger management focuses attention on the same short-circuiting strategies that most other anger management programs stress. But I add something that most other plans neglect. I try to help my client overcome all abusive behavior, beginning with selfish demands, because that's where abuse usually begins. From there, I teach a client to stop making disrespectful judgments, and then he or she is finally in a better position to get angry outbursts under control. The underlying theme of this approach to anger management is to make my client aware of the fact that he or she has no right trying to control anyone else, regardless of what that person is doing. From there we go on to create habits that take the place of demands, disrespect, and anger, so that my client can, without being controlling, get needs met by his or her spouse.

Remember, in marriage you can be your spouse's greatest source of pleasure, but you can also be your spouse's greatest source of pain, particularly if you use the stupid and abusive strategies of demands, disrespect, and anger to try to get what you need in marriage. If you use these strategies, you are almost sure to lose your spouse's love for you.

Key Principles

- You make a selfish demand when you command your spouse to do something that would benefit you at your spouse's expense, with implied threat of punishment if refused.

- You make a thoughtful request when you ask your spouse to do something for you, but withdraw it if your spouse is unwilling.

- You make a disrespectful judgment when you try to "straighten out" your spouse's attitudes, beliefs, and behavior by trying to impose on him or her your way of thinking through lecture, ridicule, threats, or other forceful means.

- You respectfully persuade your spouse when you blend your value systems, giving each one's wisdom an opportunity to override the other's foolishness.

- You have an angry outburst when you verbally or physically try to hurt your spouse because of your state of anger.

- Selfish demands, disrespectful judgments, and angry outbursts are stupid and abusive strategies to get your way through control and manipulation. They not only fail to get you what you need, but they also destroy your spouse's love for you.

Thinking It Through

1. I think you will agree with me that selfish demands are Love Busters when you are on the receiving end. They make you unhappy whenever your spouse uses them to try to get his or her way. But when you make a demand, it usually seems justified, doesn't it? That's why selfish demands are so difficult to overcome—when making one, you often think it's reasonable under the circumstances. Think of a few illustrations of demands that you and your spouse have made recently. Try to understand the perspective of the spouse making the demand and the effect it had on the spouse receiving the demand. Then think of ways you could have changed the selfish demand into a thoughtful request.

2. I believe that selfish demands should not be tolerated in marriage. Do you agree with me?

3. For the one making them, disrespectful judgments are even more difficult to recognize than are selfish demands. That's why you must rely on the reaction of your spouse to determine whether or not a comment is disrespectful. When your spouse tells you that you are being disrespectful, how do you respond? Defensively ("I didn't mean to be disrespectful," or "I'm just telling you the truth!") or constructively ("I will try not to be disrespectful to you in the future")?

4. How did you do on the Disrespectful Judgments Questionnaire? Simply put, if you try to impose your point of view on your spouse, straighten out your spouse, or express an opinion that your spouse is in some way defective, it's a disrespectful judgment. Think of a few illustrations of disrespectful judgments you and your spouse have made recently. Try to understand the perspective of the spouse making the disrespectful judgment and the effect it had on the spouse being disrespectfully judged. Then think of ways you could have changed disrespectful judgments into respectful persuasion.

5. I believe that disrespectful judgments should not be tolerated in marriage. Do you agree with me?

6. Selfish demands and disrespectful judgments are two forms of abuse in marriage. They represent ways one spouse tries to gain at the other's expense. A third form of abuse—angry outbursts—often arises when the first two are not effective. What are some of the irrational explanations you use to justify an angry outburst? Without getting into a fight, discuss with your spouse one of your recent angry outbursts and describe your irrational justification for it.

7. If either of you really believes that your angry outbursts are rationally justified, take my sincere word for it—you need professional help, because your spouse's mental and physical health is at risk. The only way you can protect each other from angry outbursts is to understand that they are never justified, regardless of what you think your spouse may have done to deserve your anger.

8. I believe that angry outbursts should never be tolerated in marriage. Do you agree with me?

chapter eleven

LOVE
BUSTERS

PART 2

The three Love Busters we just discussed—demands, disrespect, and anger—all have something in common. They are stupid attempts to get our way and they are abusive. The next two Love Busters also have something in common. They have a devastating effect on marital compatibility. If your annoying behavior is left unchecked, your habits and activities will make you impossible to live with. And if you are dishonest about what you do, because you don't want to give up your annoying activities, you develop a secret way of life that ultimately grows into a monster. Sooner or later, when this secret second life is discovered, you deal your spouse the double Love Buster of having engaged in thoughtless behavior and being dishonest about it.

> **The lifestyle you create with the decisions you make will make or break your marriage.**

The lifestyle you create with the decisions you make will make or break your marriage. If you make decisions that take each other's feelings into account, you will create a lifestyle that makes you both happy—you will have created a compatible lifestyle. But if you make thoughtless decisions or make decisions behind your spouse's back, hoping that your spouse will not discover your secrets, you will create an incompatible lifestyle, one that you and your spouse cannot enjoy together.

We are all tempted to make decisions that are in our own best interest, but not in the best interest of our spouse. And we are also tempted to keep secret any details about ourselves that reflect our weaknesses or might get us into trouble. But if spouses want to stay in love with each other, they cannot afford to tolerate these Love Busters. In the end, they will drain all the love units from your Love Banks and leave you miserable.

Annoying Behavior

When was the last time your spouse did something that annoyed you? Last week? Yesterday? An hour ago? Maybe your spouse is humming that irritating tune this very minute!

One of the most annoying things about annoying behavior is that it doesn't seem all that important—but it still drives you crazy! It's not abuse or abandonment, just annoyance. You should be able to shrug it off but you can't. It's like the steady drip-drip of water torture. Annoying behavior will nickel and dime your Love Bank into bankruptcy.

When we're annoyed, we usually consider others inconsiderate, particularly when we have explained to them that their behavior bothers us and yet they continue to do it. It's not just the behavior itself, but the thoughtlessness behind it—the idea that they just don't care. On the other hand, when our behavior annoys others, we soft-pedal the whole problem. It's just a little thing, we argue, so why make a federal case out of it? Why can't other people adjust?

> **Annoying Behavior**
>
> Habits and activities that unintentionally cause your spouse to be unhappy.

As a counselor, I try to help couples become more empathetic, to see life through each other's eyes. Of course, no one can fully imagine what someone else feels, and that's a great part of the problem. I often wish I could switch a couple's minds—Joe becomes Jane for a day and Jane becomes Joe. If they could only know what it feels like to experience their own insensitive behavior, they would change their ways in a hurry.

I've found it helpful to divide annoying behavior into two categories. If behavior is repeated without much thought, I call it an **annoying habit.** If it's usually scheduled and requires thought to complete, I call it an **annoying activity.** Annoying habits include personal mannerisms, such as the way you eat, the way you clean up after yourself (or don't!), and the way you talk. Annoying activities, on the other hand, may include sporting events you attend, your choice of church, or your personal exercise program.

> No one can fully imagine what someone else feels, and that's a great part of the problem.

Taken together, habits and activities define your entire lifestyle, and those habits and activities can be either enjoyable for both of you or enjoyable for only one of you (those that are unpleasant for both of you are usually quickly relegated to the trash bin). They are like bricks of a house, where each one is either strong or weak. The strong bricks are habits and activities that make both of you happy, while the weak bricks make one happy at the other's expense. The entire house is your lifestyle, and if it's made up of weak bricks, it is likely to collapse.

A house made up of strong bricks will make each day enjoyable for both you and your spouse, helping build your Love Bank accounts. But every annoying habit or activity drives a wedge between you and your spouse, creating and sustaining incompatibility. If you find yourselves incompatible, it's probably because there are far too many weak bricks in your marriage. Replace them as soon as possible by making an effort to eliminate annoying behavior.

But how should you go about changing your behavior so that it is no longer annoying? It begins with the realization that whenever you do something that bothers your spouse, you are withdrawing love units. Tell each other that eliminating annoying behavior is a high priority for both of you. Then ask your spouse what it is that annoys him or her the most. Write it down and go to work with a plan to eliminate it. Your spouse should do the same.

Your approach to annoying behavior should be organized with a plan to eliminate whatever it is. Unless you have such a plan that you both agree to, all you will accomplish with your criticism is a loss of love units whenever you bring up the subject.

Part 4 of this book, How to Negotiate in Marriage, addresses this very sensitive issue of eliminating annoying habits and activities, so I will leave this subject now and come back to it again later. But I want you to be aware of this fact: Unless you and your spouse change your habits and activities so that they make you both happy, instead of making only one of you happy, you will eventually find that you cannot live with each other.

Dishonesty

If your spouse had an affair ten years ago that was a brief indiscretion, would you want to know about it? If you had an affair ten years ago that you ended because you knew it was wrong, should you tell your spouse about it? These are tough questions that go to the heart of our fifth Love Buster—dishonesty.

Dishonesty is the strangest of the five Love Busters. Obviously no one likes dishonesty, but sometimes honesty seems even more damaging. What if the truth is more painful than a lie?

> **Dishonesty**
>
> Failure to reveal to your spouse correct information about your emotional reactions, personal history, daily activities, and plans for the future.

When a wife first learns that her husband has been unfaithful, the pain is often so great that she wishes she had been left ignorant. When a husband discovers his wife's affair, it's like a knife in his heart and he wonders if it would have been better not knowing. In fact many marriage counselors advise clients to avoid telling spouses about past infidelity, saying that it's too painful for people to handle. Besides, if it's over and done with, why dredge up the sewage of the past? It's this sort of advice that leads some of the most well-intentioned husbands and wives to lie to each other, or at least give each other false impressions. They feel that dishonesty will help them protect the other's feelings.

But what kind of a relationship is that? The lie is a wall that comes between the two partners, something hidden, a secret that cannot be mentioned yet is right under the surface of every conversation.

And dishonesty can be as addictive as a drug. One secret leads to another. If you start using dishonesty to protect each other's feelings, where will it end?

That's why dishonesty is a strange Love Buster. Lies clearly hurt a relationship over the long term, but truth can also hurt, especially in the short term. It's no wonder that many couples continue in dishonesty—because they feel they can't take the shock of facing the truth, at least right now. As a result, the marriage dies a slow death.

> **The lie is a wall that comes between the two partners.**

Honesty is like a flu shot. It may give you a short, sharp pain, but it keeps you healthier over the following months. In the case of infidelity, don't you think that your own affair would be one of the most important pieces of information about you? How could you ever expect to have an intimate relationship with someone to whom you cannot reveal your most inner feelings?

I'll admit that infidelity is an extreme example of something you would be tempted to lie about. But "little white lies" can be just as destructive when discovered, and there's even less justification for them. If it makes sense to be honest about something as hurtful as an affair, it makes even more sense to be honest about something more trivial, such as buying something you know your spouse would not have approved.

> **Honesty is like a flu shot. It may give you a short, sharp pain, but it keeps you healthier over the following months.**

I wanted to use the extreme case of infidelity to underscore the curious nature of this Love Buster and how important honesty is, even in extreme cases. But whether the lie is about something as devastating as an affair or something that would simply be disappointing to your spouse, it's dishonesty, not honesty, that makes matters worse.

I draw a distinction between the pain of a thoughtless act and the pain of knowing about a thoughtless act. Honesty sometimes creates some pain, the pain of knowing that your spouse has been thoughtless. But it is really the thoughtless act itself that causes the pain. Dishonesty may defer some of that pain, but it compounds the pain later. The truth usually comes out eventually, and the months or years of hiding it not only create an emotional barrier before it is revealed but also destroy trust afterward.

Dishonesty strangles compatibility. To create and sustain compatibility, you must not keep anything from your spouse. You must be honest about your thoughts, feelings, habits, likes, dislikes, personal history, daily activities, and plans for the future. When misinformation is part of the mix, you have little hope of making successful adjustments to each other. Dishonesty not only makes solutions to problems hard to find but often leaves couples ignorant of the problems themselves.

Dishonesty strangles compatibility.

There's another very important reason to be honest. Honesty tends to make our behavior more thoughtful. If we knew that everything we did and said would be televised and reviewed by all our friends, we would be far less likely to engage in thoughtless acts. Criminals would not steal and commit violent acts as much if they knew they would be caught each time they did. Honesty is the television camera in our lives. If we know that we will be honest with others about what we do, we will tend not to engage in thoughtless acts.

In an honest relationship, thoughtless acts are usually corrected. Bad habits are nipped in the bud. Honesty keeps a couple from drifting into incompatibility. As incompatible attitudes and behavior are revealed, they can become targets for elimination. But if these attitudes and behaviors remain hidden, they are left to grow out of control.

So many of the couples I've counseled have been confused as to what constitutes honesty in marriage that I have created a policy to explain it. I call it the Policy of Radical Honesty, because so many think it's radical. But from my perspective either you are honest or you are dishonest. There is no middle ground. In the next chapter, I will explain this policy to you and try to justify something so radical that there are very few counselors who recommend it. And yet, without honesty—radical honesty—your marriage has little hope for success, and you and your spouse are very unlikely to be in love with each other.

Key Principles

- If you make decisions that take each other's feelings into account, you will create a lifestyle that makes you both happy. You will have created a compatible lifestyle. But if you make thoughtless decisions, or make decisions behind your spouse's back, hoping that your spouse will not discover your secrets, you will create an incompatible lifestyle, one that you and your spouse cannot enjoy together.

- Annoying behavior is your habits and activities that unintentionally cause your spouse to be unhappy. If it's intentional, it usually falls into the category of an angry outburst.

- If your annoying behavior is repeated without much thought, it's an annoying habit. If it's usually scheduled and requires thought to complete, it's an annoying activity.

- Dishonesty is failure to reveal to your spouse correct information about your emotional reactions, personal history, daily activities, and plans for the future.

Thinking It Through

1. The first three Love Busters, selfish demands, disrespectful judgments, and angry outbursts, all have something in common. They are stupid and abusive attempts to get our way. The two Love Busters discussed in this chapter also have something in common. What is it? How does it affect the ability of you and your spouse to be in love with each other?

2. An annoying habit is behavior that is repeated without much thought. Without getting into a fight over it, discuss with your spouse recent annoying habits of both of you. Try to understand the perspective of the spouse with the annoying habit and the effect it has on the spouse finding it annoying. Then think of ways you can overcome those annoying habits. If you don't get far in your discussion, I'll give you help in the next part of this book.

3. An annoying activity is behavior that is usually scheduled and takes thought to complete. Think of some recent annoying activities of

you and your spouse. Try to understand the perspective of the spouse with the annoying activity and the effect it has on the spouse finding it annoying. Using what you have learned so far, how could you overcome these annoying activities?

4. I devote the next chapter to the subject of honesty. But before you read it, answer these questions: Do you want your spouse to be honest with you? Are you willing to be honest with your spouse? Try to understand the perspective of the spouse who has been dishonest in the past and the effect it had on the other spouse.

5. As you have read in this chapter, I am opposed to a secret second life in marriage. How do you feel about that, particularly as it relates to personal privacy? Do you think that spouses should be able to create a way of life that is separate and secret from each other or do you agree with me that everything one spouse does should be revealed to the other?

chapter twelve

THE POLICY OF RADICAL
HONESTY

Honesty is one of the ten most important emotional needs identified in marriage, which means that when it's met, it can trigger the feeling of love. Its counterpart, dishonesty, is one of the five most destructive Love Busters. When spouses are dishonest, they destroy the love they have for each other. These are two very important reasons to be honest with each other.

But there is a third reason that honesty is crucial to your marital happiness. Honesty is the only way that you and your spouse will ever come to understand each other. Without honesty, the adjustments that are crucial to the creation of compatibility in your marriage cannot be made. Without honesty, your best efforts to resolve conflicts will be wasted because you will not understand each other well enough to find mutually acceptable solutions.

> **Honesty is the only way that you and your spouse will ever come to understand each other.**

Like most couples, you probably have done your best to make each other happy, at least for a while. But your efforts, however sincere, were probably often misdirected. You were aiming at the wrong target. Ignorance, not lack of effort, is very likely the single most important reason that your marriage may not be as fulfilling as you would like it to be.

You may be ignorant not only of ways to improve your marriage but also of many of the problems themselves. To avoid conflict, you may sometimes deliberately misinform each other concerning your feelings, personal history, activities, and plans. This leads to a failure to meet an important emotional need, a withdrawal of love units when the deception is discovered, and an inability to resolve many of your marital conflicts. After all, how can you and your spouse solve a problem if one or both of you are withholding information?

To help you understand how honest you need to be to have a successful marriage, I have created the Policy of Radical Honesty. I call it "radical" because that's how many see my position on the subject. But my policy is simply advocating complete honesty in marriage. In our culture, though, I guess that's a radical idea.

Policy of Radical Honesty
Reveal to your spouse as much information about yourself as you know—your thoughts, feelings, habits, likes, dislikes, personal history, daily activities, and plans for the future.

To help explain this policy, I have broken it down into four parts. Radical honesty includes:

1. **Emotional Honesty:** Reveal your emotional reactions, both positive and negative, to the events of your life, particularly to your spouse's behavior.
2. **Historical Honesty:** Reveal information about your personal history, particularly events that demonstrate personal weakness or failure.
3. **Current Honesty:** Reveal information about the events of your day, your schedule and activities.
4. **Future Honesty:** Reveal your thoughts and plans regarding future activities and objectives.

To some extent this policy seems like motherhood and apple pie. Who would argue that it's not a good idea to be honest? But in my years of experience as a marriage counselor, I have constantly struggled with clients' belief that dishonesty can be a good idea under certain conditions. Moreover, pastors and counselors themselves often advise dishonesty when a spouse has committed a particularly thoughtless act, such as infidelity. And many marital therapists warn against complaining, something that some consider one of the seven deadly sins of marriage. So instead of complaining, spouses often stuff their feelings and try to put a good face on a bad situation.

Granted, dishonesty may look like a good short-term solution to marital conflict. It will probably get you off the hook for a few days or months or keep the problem on the back burner. But it's a terrible long-term solution. If you and your spouse expect to live with each other for the next few years and still be in love, dishonesty can get you into a great deal of trouble.

Because this is an uncommon recommendation, I will describe the four parts of my Policy of Radical Honesty one at a time, and explain to you why I think each part is so important for your marriage.

Emotional Honesty

Like so many others, you may find it difficult to openly express your negative reactions. You may fear that your response will be interpreted as criticism. Or you may feel ashamed of your own reactions, telling yourself that you should not feel the way you do. You may want unconditional acceptance from your spouse and consider that your negative reactions prove your own inability to be unconditionally accepting. Whatever the reasons, you may try to avoid expressing your negative emotional reactions.

While positive reactions are easier to communicate, you may not have learned to express these feelings, either. This failure not only misses an important opportunity to accurately communicate your basic feelings, but it also misses an opportunity to deposit love units. Whenever your spouse has made you feel good, if you express those feelings clearly and enthusiastically, you'll reward

ACTION STEP

Reveal your emotional reactions, both positive and negative, to the events of your life, particularly to your spouse's behavior.

121

your spouse for having made an appropriate adjustment to you. That, in turn, makes your spouse feel good.

If you want to meet each other's emotional needs, and you want to overcome Love Busters, one essential ingredient is an honest expression of your emotional reactions to each other. What makes a marriage successful is your willingness and ability to accommodate each other's feelings. And without the facts about those feelings, an otherwise happy couple can become very unhappy as the events of life change.

> **What makes your marriage successful is your willingness and ability to accommodate each other's feelings.**

The conditions that existed at the time of your marriage were partly responsible for the love you had for each other. Those conditions made it easy for you to meet each other's emotional needs, and tended to ward off Love Busters. They may have made you feel perfect for each other, because you did not have to do much to make each other happy.

But if you are like most couples, those conditions changed right after your marriage and have continued to change right up to the present. If you have not been able to adjust to those changes, you are probably very disillusioned about your compatibility. What had seemed effortless at first may seem impossible for you now.

But adjustment in marriage is not impossible. In fact it may be quite a bit easier than you think. Because of the way your brain is put together, you have the ability to make remarkable adjustments throughout life, as your environment changes. Besides, your behavior will change whether you determine the change or not. Will you let changing circumstances control your behavior, or will you take control yourself?

While some couples may fail to make a successful adjustment after feelings are honestly expressed, failure is almost guaranteed when the need for adjustment is never communicated. Always take each other's complaints seriously. As I mentioned earlier, your emotional reactions are a gauge of whether you are making a good adjustment to each other. If you both feel good, you need no adjustment. If one or both of you feel bad, a change is indicated.

Honesty is not demands, disrespect, or anger. Even though I have explained this before, let me explain again what honesty is not. It is not selfish demands or disrespectful judgments or angry outbursts.

Expressing a feeling is not the same as expressing demands. If you try to tell your spouse what to do, you are not revealing an honest feeling; you are making a demand. If your spouse does something that bothers you, the correct way to express it is simply to say that it bothers you.

And if you tell your spouse that he or she is wrong about something, you're not being honest; you are being disrespectful. While you should be free to express your beliefs and opinions, you should respect your spouse's beliefs and opinions if they are in conflict with yours. The expression of feeling should not carry judgmental baggage with it.

> Your emotional reactions are a gauge of whether you are making a good adjustment to each other.

It goes without saying that angry outbursts are not expressions of honesty either. When people indulge in them, they often think that they are being honest, but they are really just trying to rationalize what is actually cruel and destructive. Whatever it is you have to say when you are angry is not worth saying. Keep that basic principle in mind so that you will keep your mouth shut when you feel angry. When you have recovered from your anger, it's safe to tell your spouse what was bothering you.

To summarize, failure to express negative feelings perpetuates the withdrawal of love units. It prevents a resolution to a marital conflict, because the conflict is not expressed. Negative feelings provide evidence that you have not yet achieved a successful marital adjustment. More work is needed. Positive feelings not only offer proof of a successful adjustment, they also provide a reward to the spouse who has been successful. Don't neglect to tell each other how you feel when you are happy.

Historical Honesty

Whenever you and your spouse make a decision together or try to resolve a conflict, one factor that must never be ignored is your past. That's because mistakes and successes of the past often provide evidence of what's likely to happen in the future.

While many people feel that embarrassing experiences or serious mistakes of the past should be forgotten, most psychologists recognize that these are often signs of present weakness. For example, if someone has had an affair, he or she may be vulnerable to another one. If someone has ever been chemically dependent, he or she is vulnerable to drug or alcohol abuse in the future. By admitting your past mistakes openly, your spouse can understand your weaknesses, and together you can avoid conditions that tend to create problems for you.

No area of your life should be kept secret.

No area of your life should be kept secret. You should answer all of your spouse's questions fully and completely, with special attention given to periods of poor adjustment in your past. Not only should you explain your past to your spouse, but you should also encourage your spouse to gather information from those who knew you before you met him or her. I have encouraged couples considering marriage to meet with several significant people from each other's past. It's often a real eye-opener!

Carry this Policy of Radical Honesty about your past all the way to the disclosure of all premarital and extramarital sexual relations. Those experiences are among your most important experiences in life, and your spouse should know anything you regard as important. Past sexual experiences also create a contrast effect in marriage, and it's inevitable that you will compare your spouse sexually with all other past sexual relationships. Knowing your sexual history can make present sexual problems much easier to understand.

ACTION STEP

Reveal information about your personal history, particularly events that demonstrate personal weakness or failure.

Some of my clients have argued that if they tell their spouse about mistakes made decades earlier, their spouse will be crushed and never trust them again. Why not just leave that little demon alone? they ask.

My answer is that it's not a "little demon." If you've had an affair, it's an extremely important

124

part of your personal history, and it says something about your predispositions. Simply put, if you've had an affair in the past, your spouse shouldn't trust you—I certainly wouldn't.

But what if you haven't strayed since it happened? What if you've seen a pastor regularly to hold you accountable? Why put your spouse through the agony of a revelation that could ruin your relationship forever?

I'd say you don't give your spouse much credit! Honesty does not drive a spouse insane—dishonesty does. People in general, and women in particular, want to know exactly what their spouse is thinking and feeling. When you hold something back, your spouse tries to guess what it is. If he or she is right, then you must continually lie to cover your tracks. If he or she is wrong, an incorrect understanding of you and your predispositions develops.

> **Revealing correct information presents an opportunity for understanding and change.**

Maybe you don't really want to be known for who you are. That's the saddest position of all. You'd rather keep your secret than experience one of life's greatest joys—to be loved and accepted in spite of your weaknesses.

Some counselors argue that the only reason people reveal past infidelity is because of anger. They are deliberately trying to hurt their spouse with that information. Or they may be doing it to relieve their own guilt at the expense of their spouse's feelings.

Some of what such counselors say is true. A betrayed spouse will feel hurt. And vengeance or guilt may motivate some confessions. But revealing correct information presents an opportunity for understanding and change. And that opportunity is more important than unhealthy motives for a confession or momentary unhappiness after the confession is made.

Some revelations should be made in the presence of a professional counselor to help control the emotional damage. Spouses sometimes have difficulty adjusting to revelations that have been kept secret for years. In many cases, they're not reacting to the revelation as much as to the fact that they'd been lied to all that time.

Also, people with emotional weaknesses may need personal counseling to help them adjust to the reality of their spouse's past.

ACTION STEP

Complete a Personal History Questionnaire and write short personal histories with your spouse.

The saint they thought they married turns out to be not so saintly. But even the most negative reactions to truth that I've witnessed have never destroyed a person or a marriage. Rather it's dishonesty that destroys intimacy, the feeling of love, and ultimately marriages.

When a couple first sees me for counseling, I have them complete my Personal History Questionnaire, which systematically reviews many of the significant events of their past. I ask them to share their answers with each other and feel free to ask any questions that would be triggered by them.

I offer you and your spouse the same opportunity to investigate each other's past. I have included a copy of this questionnaire in appendix F for you to copy and complete. Make two enlarged copies, one for each of you. Leave nothing out and be willing to pursue any line of inquiry that will help you better understand each other's past.

I also encourage you to write together a short personal history of each of you. The Personal History Questionnaires you have completed will give you basic information and you can fill gaps as you ask each other questions while writing the reports. As one of you asks questions and types the history, the other simply answers the questions as honestly as possible. Then switch roles so that histories are written for both of you.

Not only will these short personal histories help you know each other and understand each other better, but they will become invaluable later on when your children and grandchildren want to know something about your lives.

Current Honesty

In good marriages, couples become so interdependent that sharing a daily schedule is essential to their coordination of activities. But in weak marriages, couples are reluctant to provide their schedules, because they are often engaged in an assortment of Love Busters. They may know that their spouse would object to their activities, so they tell themselves, *What my spouse doesn't know won't hurt.* They have what I call a "secret second life."

There are also those who really have nothing to hide, yet they feel the need for privacy. They are offended when their spouse asks where they've been or what they've done. They believe their spouse should trust them and not assume the worst. I believe they are wrong, because privacy creates an unnecessary barrier to problem solving.

When you and your spouse married, two became one. Prior to marriage, you had no one but yourself to consider when you made choices, but now you have each other to consider. There should be no part of your life that is off-limits to your spouse, because literally everything that either of you do will ultimately affect each other. Privacy breeds incompatibility because it creates a part of your life that is off-limits to accommodation.

> **ACTION STEP**
>
> Reveal information about the events of your day. Provide your spouse with a calendar of your activities, with special emphasis on those that may affect your spouse.

> **Privacy breeds incompatibility.**

Even when activities are innocent, it's extremely important for your spouse to understand what you do with your time. Be easy to check up on and find in an emergency. Give each other your daily schedules so you can communicate about how you spend your time. Since almost everything you do will affect your spouse, it's important to explain what it is you do.

Honesty is a terrific way to protect each other from potentially damaging activities. Knowing that you'll be telling each other everything you've been up to, you're far less likely to get into trouble.

Future Honesty

After having made such a big issue of revealing past indiscretions, you can imagine how I feel about revealing future plans. They're much easier to discuss with your spouse, yet many couples make plans independently of each other. Some couples don't explain their plans because they don't want to change them, even if their spouse expresses negative reactions. They feel that explaining a future plan may cause a battle, and their spouse will successfully scuttle the plan. And some don't explain their future plans because they don't think their spouse would be interested. They think there's nothing upsetting about the plan, so there'd be no point in revealing it.

Even if your plans are innocent, failing to tell your spouse your future plans is being dishonest. You don't really know what your spouse's reaction will be, and by failing to give advance notice, you may create a problem for the future. Besides, if you and your spouse are partners in life, your plans are important to both of you, whether your spouse feels that way or not.

You may believe your plans are best for both you and your spouse and, once your spouse sees the plan succeed, he or she will be grateful that you went ahead with it. Or you may feel that if you wait for your spouse's approval, you will never accomplish anything. Perhaps your spouse is so conservative that if you wait for his or her approval, you think you'll miss every opportunity that comes your way.

> In good marriages, couples share information about daily activities.

Regardless of how you feel about revealing your plans, failure to do so will leave your spouse in the dark. While no love units are withdrawn at the time you're deceitful, they will almost surely be withdrawn when your spouse realizes you've held back information. It also sets up the loss of more love units if your plan fails to take your spouse's feelings into account.

Since your schedule each week is part of your future plans, every hour you schedule should be discussed with your spouse before you firm it up. How many hours of waking time do you have at your disposal? Do you schedule any or all of that time? Do you and your spouse share your weekly schedules with each other before you commit yourselves to that time? I suggest that every Sunday afternoon at 3:30, you and your spouse set aside one-half hour to go over your schedules for the coming week. That way you will know what each of you is doing that week, and you will have an opportunity to change any part of the schedule as needed.

ACTION STEP

Reveal your thoughts and plans regarding future activities and objectives.

It makes sense for you to discuss your schedule on a daily basis, so that each new item can be reviewed as it comes along. But the reason that I suggest a final review on Sunday afternoon is to get you into the habit of giving each other a chance to veto anything in either of your schedules that does not have your enthusiastic agreement. Get used to the idea that you simply should not do something that your spouse does not like. And give your spouse an opportunity to react to whatever it is you are planning to do.

I hope that I have been able to convince you that radical honesty is essential for a great marriage. I have devoted an entire chapter to this issue because there are so many cultural forces that will try to convince you otherwise. If you discuss my arguments with each other, I think you will eventually agree with me that dishonesty is a Love Buster, and radical honesty is its only reasonable alternative.

> ## ACTION
> # STEP
>
> Discuss your weekly plans with your spouse every Sunday afternoon at 3:30.

> **Get used to the idea that you simply should not do something that your spouse does not like.**

Follow Through

Step 1: Radical Honesty—Review the three reasons I believe radical honesty is important in marriage. Then consider what instincts and behaviors make radical honesty difficult. Look for ways in which they have prevented you from being honest in the past, and determine to overcome those instincts and habits to be honest in the future.

Step 2: Emotional Honesty—Think of recent instances when either of you have been unable to honestly express your emotional reactions. Try to understand the perspective of the spouse having trouble being honest about his or her emotional reactions and the effect it has on the other spouse. Then think of ways you can become honest about your emotional reactions.

Step 3: Historical Honesty—Make two copies and complete the Personal History Questionnaire that I have provided in appendix F. Exchange the questionnaires so that you can learn more about each other's past. Then interview each other so that you can learn even more about each other. For extra credit, write a short biography of each other based on the information you gleaned from the questionnaires and your interviews. Then update your biographies every five years. They will become a treasure to your descendants for generations to come.

Step 4: Current Honesty—Provide your spouse with a calendar of your activities, with special emphasis on those activities that may affect your spouse. I suggest that you carry a cell phone so that you can always reach each other in an emergency. Don't allow any part of your life to be kept secret from each other, and encourage each other to investigate your lives as much as possible. Discuss ways that you can both become more aware of each other's daily activities.

Step 5: Future Honesty—Get into the habit of sharing your weekly schedules with each other every Sunday afternoon at 3:30. It will not only help you coordinate your activities, but it will also help you think of each other when you make future plans. Spend time each week talking to each other about your hopes and dreams, and what you can do to make them become a reality. Even if your future plans are never implemented, discussing them will help you get to know each other much better. What obstacles would prevent you from expressing your future plans with each other? How can you avoid those obstacles?

IDENTIFYING AND
OVERCOMING
L O V E   B U S T E R S

Wouldn't it be great if from now on you and your spouse never intentionally hurt each other? Or if when one of you hurt the other by mistake, you immediately apologized and took steps to avoid doing it again?

Failure to protect your spouse from your own selfish habits and instincts is a greater disaster in marriage than the failure to care for your spouse. Once you unleash pain on your spouse, his or her desire to meet your emotional needs evaporates. There's no point in discussing emotional needs as long as Love Busters dominate a relationship. When a person is in pain, he or she is in no mood to meet needs or have them met.

That's why a willingness to care is often negated by an unwillingness to protect. Many couples who come to me for counseling have stopped caring for each other because Love Busters have made care disappear. Not only do Love Busters withdraw love units that were deposited by meeting emotional needs, but they also prevent more love units from being deposited—they stop care right in its tracks.

> **Failure to protect your spouse from your own selfish habits and instincts is a greater disaster in marriage than the failure to care for your spouse.**

It's of critical importance to root out Love Busters if you want to keep your Love Bank balances high.

Love Busters don't belong in your marriage. Whatever excuse you may have to tolerate them, it can never justify the damage they do. Angry outbursts, disrespectful judgments, annoying behavior, selfish demands, dishonesty—every one of them will hurt your love for each other because when you do any of them, you are hurting each other.

Love Busters usually don't enter a relationship with a full-scale invasion. They often begin with a seemingly harmless foothold. But from this inauspicious beginning, they grow to become ugly, destructive habits that can ruin your marriage.

> **The person on the receiving end of these Love Busters has to identify them, because that person is the one who feels the pain.**

If you have allowed Love Busters to gain a foothold, but they have not had a chance to grow very much, you may not see them as the monsters they really are. But if you have been living with them for a while, I'm sure you will have no argument with my basic premise that they ruin marriages.

I suggest you follow a four-step plan to help you identify and eliminate any Love Busters that have nosed their way into your relationship. If you find any, this plan will help you eliminate them quickly so they don't grow to do serious damage. But even if damage has already been done, there's no time like the present to usher them to the door. And once they are out in the cold, you and your spouse can begin to warm up your relationship with the love you both should have for each other.

ACTION STEP

Use the Love Busters Questionnaire to identify the Love Busters affecting your relationship.

Step 1: Identify Love Busters

Before you go to battle, you need to know your enemy. And if you're battling Love Busters, you need to know how they express themselves. I have identified five broad types of Love Busters that can turn us all into monsters, but which of these are especially threatening to your marriage, and what specific behavior is involved?

One spouse is often ignorant of the things he or she does to hurt the other. Love Busters can become second nature—habits we don't even think about. The perpetrator often doesn't even remember doing them. That's why the person on the receiving end of these Love Busters has to identify them, because that person is the one who feels the pain. You must tell each other what makes you unhappy.

Focus immediate attention on the Love Buster that is causing the most damage.

If you would like to identify Love Busters that are responsible for Love Bank withdrawals in your relationship, make two enlarged copies of the Love Busters Questionnaire (appendix G). Both you and your spouse should complete a questionnaire.

None of us likes to be criticized, and when we are, we often react defensively. If you are not careful, you may respond to your spouse's revelations with anger and disrespect, especially if you have not learned to overcome those Love Busters in your marriage.

So when you read each other's questionnaires, be careful to accept the evaluation with your spouse's protection in mind. Your questionnaires will help you discover areas where your protection needs improvement. You may be offended by what you read, but an honest assessment of your conduct is essential information that will help you do a better job protecting each other.

Step 2: Rank Love Busters

In some marriages, all five types of Love Busters ruin the relationship. But for most, it's only two or three that cause most of the damage. Whether all five are present, or only two, it makes sense to focus immediate attention on the one that's the worst. Once you are on your way to eliminating that one, you can turn your energy and attention to the next most troublesome Love Buster.

ACTION STEP

Rank all five Love Busters in terms of impact.

I suggest that you focus your attention on only one, or possibly two, Love Busters at a time. That way you will be successful in defeating the greatest enemies of your relationship. Once they are overcome, you can then address the others. If you try to defeat several at the same time, you will probably not be successful.

Focus immediate attention on the Love Buster that's the worst.

To help you choose which Love Buster should be tackled first, you and your spouse must rank each other's Love Busters in terms of their impact on your relationship. Decide which Love Buster causes the greatest unhappiness and rank that number one. Continue ranking the Love Busters on the list until you have ranked them all.

Step 3: Agree to Eliminate Love Busters for Each Other

It's easy for you to understand why your spouse should change to protect you, but it's usually more difficult to understand why you should change to protect your spouse. However, if you have promised to protect each other, it's essential that you believe each other's assertion that changes are necessary.

ACTION STEP

Complete the Agreement to Overcome Love Busters.

As a concrete act of protection, I suggest that you make a commitment with each other to eliminate the Love Busters that either of you have identified. To help formalize your intentions, I have prepared an Agreement to Overcome Love Busters (appendix H). It provides space for you and your spouse to list the Love Busters you will eliminate for each other's protection.

Step 4: Overcome the Love Busters

In some cases, the decision to avoid a Love Buster is all it takes. For example, most annoying activities can be overcome when you remove them from your schedule. And some people are so disciplined that even long-held habits can be eliminated with a decision, but for most people, a plan must be created to eliminate the old habit and create a new habit. And there should be someone to hold you accountable to complete the plan. If you find that you continue to hurt your spouse after you have made a reasonable effort to overcome a Love Buster, you may need professional help.

ACTION STEP

Develop a plan for overcoming Love Busters, using additional resources as needed.

Marriage support groups sponsored by church or community organizations may enable you to overcome Love Busters by being accountable to others in the group. Individuals in the group check up on their members, holding them to their promises. Or you may choose to ask a marriage counselor to hold you accountable. Marriage counselors are trained to monitor your progress and remind you of your commitment. But be certain that the counselor you choose is experienced and effective in eliminating the Love Buster that is hurting your marriage. And be sure that the counselor is able to eliminate it quickly. If one counselor does not seem to be helping you make progress, find another.

Make eliminating Love Busters your highest priority. They should not be allowed to exist in your marriage because they do so much damage. If your relationship is to survive, you must root them out as soon as possible.

If you would like to read more on this subject, I suggest you read my book *Love Busters: Overcoming Habits That Destroy Romantic Love.* Its accompanying workbook, *Five Steps to Romantic Love,* contains worksheets to help you create an effective plan to keep those rascals from ruining your marriage.

And then, if you need special motivation, I have prepared an audio series, *Love Busters: Overcoming Habits That Destroy Passion* that provides eight weekly lessons that guide you through the chapters of *Love Busters* and the worksheets in *Five Steps to Romantic Love.*

As I mentioned when discussing annoying behavior, it's essential for you and your spouse to create a compatible lifestyle, free of annoying habits and activities, a living environment that makes you both happy. But creating that compatible lifestyle is quite a challenge for most couples, so I will use part 4 of this book to show you how it's done.

Follow Through

Step 1: Copy and enlarge the Love Busters Questionnaire (appendix G). Each of you complete one questionnaire so that you can identify Love Busters that are responsible for Love Bank withdrawals.

Step 2: To help you choose which Love Buster should be tackled first, rank each other's Love Busters in terms of their impact on your relationship. Decide which Love Buster causes the greatest unhappiness and rank that 1. Continue ranking the Love Busters on the list until you have ranked them all.

Step 3: As a concrete act of protection, make a commitment to each other to eliminate the Love Busters that either of you have identified. To help formalize your intentions, list the Love Busters you have identified in the space provided for you in Agreement to Overcome Love Busters (appendix H).

Step 4: Create a plan to overcome the Love Busters that threaten your love for each other.

Step 5: Implement your plan until the Love Busters are eliminated.

Additional Resources

Willard F. Harley, Jr. *Love Busters: Overcoming Habits that Destroy Romantic Love.* Grand Rapids: Revell, 1992, 1997. The five most common, but dangerous, ways that spouses hurt each other and how to avoid them: selfish demands, disrespectful judgments, angry outbursts, annoying behavior, and dishonesty.

Willard F. Harley, Jr. *Five Steps to Romantic Love.* Grand Rapids: Revell, 1993. A workbook to accompany *Love Busters* that contains the worksheets that I use in my practice to help couples learn how to eliminate Love Busters in their marriage.

Willard F. Harley, Jr. *Love Busters: Overcoming Habits That Destroy Passion.* St. Paul: Marriage Builders, 2000. This audio series helps motivate you to avoid the habits that are the most dangerous in marriage. It comes with the book *Love Busters* and the workbook *Five Steps to Romantic Love.* To order this audio series, call Marriage Builders at 1-888-639-1639.

part four

HOW TO
NEGOTIATE
IN MARRIAGE

chapter fourteen

THE GIVER AND
THE TAKER

Some of my clients are professional negotiators, and some lead seminars on how to negotiate. You'd think these experts would have the inside track when it comes to bargaining with their spouse. But they don't. That's because there's something about marital negotiation that leaves even the experts looking like idiots.

I've seen this happen in case after case. An intelligent man listens to his wife talking about her needs, her desires, her interests, and it's as if she's speaking a foreign language. Likewise, a brilliant woman hears her husband describe his perspective, and she just doesn't get it.

What makes marital negotiation so tough? Is it that men and women just can't communicate? Or is there something about marriage that blurs their thinking?

> The Giver and the Taker make marital problem solving much more difficult than it should be.

Having spent decades counseling couples that seem communicationally challenged, I am thoroughly convinced that it is marriage itself (or more specifically, a romantic relationship)—not differences between men and women—that makes communication difficult. The men I counsel have very little trouble resolving conflicts with women, and their wives are usually just as good at negotiating with men. It's only the conflicts they have with their spouse that seem impossible to resolve.

Part of the problem lies with the very nature of our personalities. Have you ever suspected your spouse of having not one but two personalities—one that is caring and considerate and one that seems impossible to get along with? You've probably not only noticed but also been terrorized by the impossible one. Both personalities are alive and well in each of us. I call these two personalities the Giver and the Taker, and they are responsible for making marital problem solving much more difficult than it should be.

To help you understand why it's so tough to communicate in marriage, and why it's so hard to be consistently kind and considerate, I'll explain to you who these characters are and how they influence our thinking when we are faced with marital conflict.

Getting to Know Your Giver

The Giver is the part of you that follows this rule: *Do whatever you can to make the **other person** happy and avoid anything that makes the **other person** unhappy, even if it makes you unhappy.* It's the part of you that wants to make a difference in the lives of others, and it grows out of a basic instinct that we all share, a deep reservoir of love and concern for those around us.

> **The Giver wants you to meet the needs of others but is not concerned about your needs.**

If your Giver had its way, plaques would cover your walls, proclaiming such messages as, "Love Unconditionally," "Live for the Joy of Making Someone Happy," and "Don't Think of Yourself, Think of Others." You see, it's the Giver's mission in life to help as many people as possible without consideration for self. The Giver is not concerned about being repaid for services rendered. In fact the Giver feels that it's more important to help those who cannot repay than to help those who would reciprocate.

The Giver wants you to make a constructive difference in the lives of others during your lifetime and wants you to do it without thought for yourself. In short, the Giver's goal in life is to make others happy, even if it's at your expense. The Giver wants you to meet the needs of others but is not concerned about your needs.

Everyone has a Giver. Even the cruelest terrorist is fighting for a cause he thinks will ease the suffering of those he cares for. Some of the most evil, sociopathic people I've ever known have had a compassionate, loving side. That's why some murderers, rapists, and child molesters can appear to be rehabilitated. They sincerely want—at least some of the time—to avoid ever hurting anyone again.

> **The Giver**
>
> This is the part of you that follows the rule: Do whatever you can to make the other person happy and avoid anything that makes the other person unhappy, even if it makes you unhappy.

I've been intrigued by those who choose marriage partners with serious social and physical limitations—alcoholics, addicts, criminals, the chronically unemployed. They seem to be attracted to the obvious needs of the individual. Why? It's the Giver within them.

The Giver is looking for someone to care for. So being needed is a powerful reason to marry, because the Giver in each of us wants to provide care for one special person. I know that's why I married Joyce, and she felt the same way toward me.

> **The Giver is looking for someone to care for.**

But the Giver is only half of the story. There is another personality that also has a great influence on our decisions. It's the Taker.

Getting to Know Your Taker

Just as your Giver tries to make others happy or tries to prevent the suffering of others, your Taker tries to make you happy and tries to prevent your suffering. It's the part of you that follows this rule: *Do whatever you can to make **you** happy and avoid anything that makes **you** unhappy, even if it makes others unhappy.* It's the part of you that wants you to get the most out of life, and it grows out of your basic instinct for self-preservation.

I've found that even those who appear to be the most self-sacrificing have a Taker lurking in the background. If you've ever worked with those who dedicated their lives to the welfare of others—social workers, disaster-relief volunteers, missionaries, and yes, even psychologists—you know they are not totally selfless. They have a Taker too.

If the Taker had its way, your walls would be covered with plaques reading, "What's in It for Me?" and "Self-esteem Is the Greatest Virtue." The Taker is not interested in the happiness of others and is quite willing for you to gain at the expense of others. In fact it encourages you to do that very thing. The Taker's mission in life is to make you, and only you, happy and safe. It is your advocate and your defense attorney—your best friend.

> **The Taker**
>
> This is the part of you that follows the rule: Do whatever you can to make you happy and avoid anything that makes you unhappy, even if it makes others unhappy.

Marriage is viewed by your Taker as an opportunity to have some of your most important emotional needs met. In selecting a spouse, your Taker considers all the pluses and minuses. What will you get, and what will you be expected to give? It wants you to strike a good bargain—and for the Taker that means getting as much as possible for as little as possible.

Your Love Bank balances are very important to your Taker because they reflect how much happiness you receive from people. Your Taker wants you to marry the one with the largest Love Bank account, because that's the person who makes you the happiest. But it isn't concerned about anyone else's Love Bank. If someone doesn't give you enough, your Taker wants you to force that person to give you more, or find someone else to give you what you want.

> **The Taker's mission in life is to make you, and only you, happy and safe.**

Your Taker thinks that the Giver's idea of unconditional love is great, as long as it's the other person who loves *you* unconditionally. It likes the freedom of getting your needs met with no strings attached. But it will strongly advise you not to care for someone else unconditionally.

Like so many others, when you went to the altar, you promised to have and to hold your spouse from that day forward, for better or for worse, in sickness and in health, to love and to cherish, until you are parted by death— as God was your witness you gave your promise. Yet more than half of the couples that make those vows divorce, and two-thirds of those that remain married for life report an absence of love and cherishing. The vow doesn't seem to mean much to people. Do you know why? It's because their Taker never agreed to it in the first place. It's a Giver's vow, not a Taker's vow. And if you ever file for divorce, it's your Taker that is encouraging you to do it.

> **Your Taker thinks that the Giver's idea of unconditional love is great, as long as it's the other person who loves *you* unconditionally.**

Your Shortsighted Giver and Taker

It's tempting to consider the Giver as our caring nature and the Taker as our thoughtless nature. But that's not what they are. Actually, they are both caring—your Giver cares for others and your Taker cares for you.

Both Giver and Taker also have their thoughtless sides. Your Giver does not care how you feel, and your Taker does not care how others feel. In fact your Giver is willing to see you suffer, even to the point of deep depression, as long as you continue to care about others. Your Taker, on the other hand, is willing to see others suffer if it means that you are happy or are prevented from suffering.

> **Your Giver and Taker are both good and bad.**

The truth is, your Giver and Taker are both good and bad. They are good because they both care, the Giver for others and the Taker for you. But they are bad because they are both thoughtless, the Giver caring nothing for your feelings and the Taker caring nothing for the feelings of others. Because each of them ignores someone's feelings, they are both shortsighted. The Giver and Taker fail to understand that you and others should be cared for and protected simultaneously, so that no one suffers.

145

There is something else that neither your Giver nor your Taker understands—we are more motivated to meet the needs of someone else (satisfying the Giver) when our own needs are being met by that person (satisfying the Taker). And we are more effective in motivating someone else to meet our needs when we meet his or her needs.

Reciprocity is essential for the survival of any relationship.

We really can't meet our own most important emotional needs. Affection, conversation, recreational companionship, sexual fulfillment, honesty and openness, physical attractiveness, financial support, domestic support, family commitment, admiration—these are all needs that can be met only by someone else. And no one will meet our needs for long if we are not meeting their needs. Reciprocity is essential for the survival of any relationship. It requires both give and take.

How Your Giver and Taker Resolve Marital Conflict

In everyday life, our Giver and Taker usually solve problems together. Our intelligence, which usually overrides the shortsighted interests of the Giver and Taker, recognizes our need to give and take simultaneously. For example, when we buy groceries, we give money and take groceries. We don't give more money than the grocer charges us and we don't take groceries without paying for them.

But in marriage, a strange thing happens to the way our Giver and Taker operate. They seem to work independently of each other. Either the Giver is in charge, and we give unconditionally to our spouse; or the Taker is in charge, and we take what we want from our spouse without giving anything in return. Our intelligence seems to turn decision making over to either our Giver or Taker. And that strategy has disastrous consequences because fair negotiation, which requires give *and* take, is impossible.

When the Giver is in charge of our decisions, we are loving and considerate but we tend to make personal sacrifices to see to it that our spouse is happy and fulfilled. This can happen because our Taker is not there to defend our personal interests and our Giver does not care how we feel.

146

But when the Taker is in charge, we are rude, demanding, and inconsiderate. All we seem to think about is ourselves, and what our spouse can do to make us happy. We expect our spouse to make sacrifices for us, because our Taker doesn't care how our spouse feels.

I want to emphasize to you that this is normal behavior in marriage. You may think you're married to a crazy person, or you may think you're crazy yourself, but let me assure you, marriage is one of the very few relationships that bring out the pure Giver and Taker in each of us. And that usually makes us seem much crazier than we really are.

> **Marriage is one of the very few relationships that bring out the pure Giver and Taker in each of us.**

Why is this true? Is there something that sets us up for all this craziness? I believe that the culprit is the intensity of emotional reactions that are created in all romantic relationships. To reap the rewards of romantic ecstasy, we open a Pandora's box of emotions. The emotional reaction we want, of course, is the feeling of romantic love. But when we open ourselves up to experience that feeling, we become vulnerable to a greater intensity of all the opposite feelings, too—anger, fear, and hopelessness.

That's why it is so important for you to understand how to keep your Love Bank balances high. As long as you keep depositing love units in each other's Love Bank, and avoid withdrawing them, you will experience everything a marriage is supposed to be. But if you let those balances fall, your negative emotional reactions will hit you like a ton of bricks.

So the reason your Giver and Taker play such a prominent role in your marital relationship is that you have more intense emotions to deal with than you do in your interactions with other people around you. Your Giver and Taker reflect the purely emotional side of you. But if you want your marriage to thrive, you must use your intelligence to rein them in, or they will ruin your marriage.

It should be no surprise to you that it isn't the Giver that does the most to ruin your marriage—it's the Taker. But the Giver plays a very important role in creating the problem. It's the effort of the Giver to give your spouse anything he or she wants that sets up the Taker for its destructive acts. After you have been giving, giving, giving to your spouse, and receiving little in return (because you haven't asked for much), your Taker rises up to straighten out the situation. It sees the unfairness of it all and steps in to balance the books. But instead of coming to a more balanced arrangement, where you get something for what you give, the Taker just moves the Giver out of the picture altogether. It says, "I've been giving enough; now it's your turn to give."

Sound familiar? We've all been through it, but it doesn't work. All your Taker does is rouse your spouse's Taker, and before you can say, "Bull in a china closet," you're having a fight.

This brings up a very important observation: The Taker's instinctive strategy for getting what you need in marriage is to make demands, show disrespect, and have an angry outburst. Does that also sound familiar? Those are the stupid and abusive instincts that I call Love Busters. And that's precisely what the Taker usually does when given control of your marriage. It ruins the love you and your spouse have for each other.

But I'm getting a little ahead of myself. Before you can fully understand how your Taker makes you argue instead of negotiate, I need to explain how the Giver and Taker take over all of your negotiations in marriage by creating what I call the Three States of Mind in Marriage.

Key Principles

- The Giver is the part of you that follows this rule: Do whatever you can to make the other person happy and avoid anything that makes the other person unhappy, even if it makes you unhappy.

- The Taker is the part of you that follows this rule: Do whatever you can to make you happy and avoid anything that makes you unhappy, even if it makes others unhappy.

- Your Giver and Taker are both good and bad. They are good because they both care, the Giver for others and the Taker for you. But they are bad because they are both thoughtless, the Giver caring nothing for your feelings and the Taker caring nothing for the feelings of others.

- Marriage is one of the very few relationships that bring out the pure Giver and Taker in each of us. And that usually makes us seem much crazier than we really are.

- We are more effective in meeting the needs of others (satisfying the Giver) when our own needs are being met (satisfying the Taker). And we are more effective in having our own needs met by others when we meet their needs. Reciprocity is necessary for the survival of any romantic relationship.

Thinking It Through

1. Before you read this chapter, had you already come to the conclusion that your spouse had two sides to him or her—a caring and generous side and a thoughtless and selfish side? If so, what was it about your spouse's behavior that led you to that conclusion?

2. What are some of the ways your spouse's Giver behaves? How does your spouse's Taker tend to behave? Most people recognize them in their spouse but have a more difficult time seeing them in themselves. Do you see the Giver and Taker in yourself as easily as you can see them in your spouse?

3. Discuss unconditional love with each other. The Giver believes that what you give to your spouse should be self-sacrificing and unconditional. What does that mean in practice? When your care is not reciprocated by your spouse's care for you, do you think that's fair?

4. Your Taker is as unconditionally taking as your Giver is unconditionally giving. Have you ever felt that since you have already given to your spouse unconditionally, it's time for you to take what you need from your spouse unconditionally? Can you see why that approach to negotiation won't work?

5. How are the Giver and Taker both caring and thoughtless? If your feelings are as important as your spouse's feelings, why should you and your spouse resist some of the advice of both your Givers and Takers?

6. How do your Giver and Taker try to resolve conflicts in your marriage? Illustrate with a recent conflict. When you were trying to
resolve it, did you use any of the stupid and abusive instincts of the
Taker? Would you like to override those instincts with a more intelligent and effective approach?

chapter fifteen

THE THREE STATES
OF MIND
IN MARRIAGE

Marriages or, to be more precise, romantic relationships are powered by emotion. The emotion we most commonly associate with marriage is love because that's what motivates couples to marry each other. But sadly, after the wedding, there are more couples who hate each other than who love each other. That's because emotions rather than intelligence usually dominate the way couples tend to solve problems, and when emotions are in control, problems are rarely solved.

> **Marriages or, to be more precise, romantic relationships are powered by emotion.**

In marriage, even though we may try to analyze our marital problems rationally, our feelings come crashing through, distorting our perception and twisting our logic. Marital disputes strike us at the core of our being, shaking our dreams, our expectations, and our sense of fairness. As a result, instead of reacting to these disputes calmly and with measured reason, we react emotionally.

It's as if you are on a roller coaster, high one second, low the next. Just when you begin to level off, you go into another dive.

And it's hard to hold an intelligent conversation on a roller coaster. Go to an amusement park and listen: What do you hear? Unintelligible screams.

That's basically what I hear in a lot of the marriage counseling I do—screams of uncertainty and fear. *Where are we going? What are we doing? I don't know what to expect from you anymore!*

Before they can make sound decisions and reasonable progress, couples desperately need to get off the roller coaster and plant their feet on solid ground. But that's easier said than done. How can a couple get control of their emotional reactions long enough to use their intelligence and solve their problems? I will give you the answer to that question in the remainder of this book. And it's an extremely valuable lesson to learn. But first, I will introduce you to the way couples tend to negotiate while on the roller coaster.

My experience trying to help couples negotiate has led me to the conclusion that, left to their own devices, couples negotiate from one of three states of mind, each having its own unique negotiating rules and its own unique emotional reactions. I call these states of mind *intimacy, conflict,* and *withdrawal.* And regardless of which state spouses are in, negotiations can be very difficult, because in each case, emotional reactions tend to override intelligence.

The First State of Mind: Intimacy

The most essential prerequisite for the *state of intimacy* is the feeling of being in love. As I discussed in the section on the Love Bank, you have that feeling when your spouse has deposited enough love units into his or her account in your Love Bank to trigger that reaction.

> **State of Intimacy**
> The state of mind dominated by your Giver, who encourages you to give unconditionally.

In this most enjoyable state of a relationship, you put your Giver in charge of decision making and follow the rule of the Giver: *Do whatever you can to make **your spouse** happy, and avoid anything that makes **your spouse** unhappy, even if it makes **you** unhappy.* When both you and your spouse are in the state of intimacy, you both follow this rule and you both usually get your emotional needs met. All is well with the world.

In this state of mind, since the Giver is in charge, giving to each other seems almost instinctive. Both you and your spouse have a great desire to make each other happy in any way you can, and you want to avoid hurting each other at all costs.

As you protect each other, trust builds. You can share your deepest feelings and become emotionally vulnerable because you know that you both have each other's best interests at heart. You feel so close to each other that to hurt the other person would be the same as hurting yourself.

Conversation in the state of intimacy is respectful and non-judgmental. You express your deepest love for each other and gratitude for the care you are receiving. By lowering your defenses and forming a close emotional bond, you feel great pleasure when you meet each other's needs. This is the way everyone wants their marriage to be.

The Giver rules negotiation in this state of marriage. When one spouse expresses a desire, the other rushes to fulfill it. There is no thought of repayment because the Giver's care is unconditional. And as long as both spouses are in the same state of mind, there is actually nothing to negotiate. They give each other anything that's possible, and they do it unconditionally.

But as I already mentioned, giving unconditionally isn't really negotiating. It's giving whatever is requested without wanting anything in return. And more important, it's giving with the attitude that bargaining would be immoral because it would imply conditions.

You can get into some very bad habits when you are in the state of intimacy. A new mother in love with her husband may let her husband completely off the hook when it comes to child care. A husband in love with his wife may do nothing to restrain her tendency toward irresponsible spending, driving them both into bankruptcy. And once these bad habits have been around for a while, they are very difficult to change.

You'd think that the state of intimacy would guide a husband and wife toward marital bliss. But, instead, because of the

Giver's failure to negotiate terms that benefit both spouses, it tends to drive them toward the second state of mind in marriage—*conflict.*

The Second State of Mind: Conflict

As long as you and your spouse are happy, the state of intimacy hums right along. But no one is happy all the time, especially when making sacrifices to make someone else happy. And when either you or your spouse experiences unhappiness, your slumbering Taker is immediately alerted to the pain. "What's going on? Who's upsetting you and why?" your Taker wants to know.

> **State of Conflict**
>
> The state of mind dominated by your Taker, who encourages you to take unconditionally.

It can be a temporary lapse if your spouse is still in a giving mood and apologizes for the error (whether or not it's his or her fault). Your spouse may promise to be more thoughtful in the future or make a greater effort to meet an unmet need. If your Taker is satisfied that all is well, and goes back to sleep, leaving the Giver in charge, you will remain in the state of Intimacy.

But what happens if there are no apologies? What if the damage is not repaired quickly? What if your spouse is unable to meet an emotional need? When that occurs, your Taker, mindful of all of your sacrifices, comes to your defense.

"I think it's time for a new rule," the Taker advises. "You've done enough giving for a while, now it's time to get something in return." You agree and decide to put your Taker in charge of decision making, following the Taker's rule: *Do whatever you can to make **you** happy, and avoid anything that makes **you** unhappy, even if it makes **your spouse** unhappy.* Giving unconditionally is replaced by taking unconditionally. When that happens, you've entered the second state of mind in marriage—*conflict.*

When you follow the Taker's rule, it isn't long before your spouse's Taker convinces him or her that it's time for a change of leadership too. The remaining Giver is pushed aside and now your spouse is ready for battle. In this state of conflict, neither of you is willing to be thoughtful or to meet each other's needs. Instead, you demand that the other spouse become more thoughtful and that your own needs be met first. You no longer guarantee each other protection but threaten each other unless your demands are met. When demands are not met, the Taker resorts to disrespectful judgments, and when that doesn't work, out come the armaments. Angry outbursts are the Taker's last-ditch effort to solve the problem.

In the state of conflict, conversation tends to be disrespectful, resentful, and even hateful. Mutual care and concern are replaced with mutual self-centeredness. Your Taker no longer trusts your spouse to look after your interests and pulls out all the stops to force him or her to treat you "fairly." The problem, of course, is that your Taker does not know how to treat your spouse with that same fairness. Fairness, according to your Taker, is getting *your* way.

> You can return to the state of intimacy from the state of conflict if, and only if, you stop hurting each other and return to meeting each other's emotional needs again.

In the state of conflict, you are still emotionally bonded to each other, and that makes the pain of thoughtlessness even worse. Love Bank withdrawals are made at a very rapid rate. You may both still hope that the hurting will stop and there will be a return to the state of intimacy, but you don't trust each other to stop the madness. You can return to the state of intimacy from the state of conflict if, and only if, you stop hurting each other and return to meeting each other's emotional needs again.

But it's very difficult to be thoughtful in the state of conflict because your Taker urges you to return pain whenever you receive it. So the state of conflict inspires you to be shortsighted. Instead of wanting to meet each other's needs, you want your own needs met before you will do anything. That makes resolving the conflict seem almost impossible, because your Takers would rather fight than try to make each other happy.

Negotiations in the state of intimacy don't take place because each of you is trying to out-give each other. However, negotiations in the state of conflict don't take place either. Each of you is trying to out-take the other. There is no effort to make the other spouse happy, only the self-centered effort of pleasing yourself at the other person's expense.

When you're in the state of conflict, your Taker, by making demands, showing disrespect, and threatening your spouse with angry outbursts to get its way, tries to force your spouse to meet your needs. If you are in the state of conflict long enough, the resentment and disillusionment you experience eventually convince your Taker that fighting doesn't work. A new approach is warranted, and the Taker has a suggestion that ushers in the third state of mind in marriage—*withdrawal.*

The Third State of Mind: Withdrawal

Reason would dictate that demands, disrespect, and anger are not the way to resolve conflicts in marriage. But with the Giver and Taker in charge, reason doesn't play a role in marital problem solving. Instead, emotion is almost everything, and after a fight, most couples do not feel much like going back to the rule of the Giver. "After all," their Takers argue, "why reward bad behavior?"

So they leave their Taker in charge, and they adopt a new approach. In the state of conflict, its strategy is **fight**. But in the state of withdrawal, its strategy is **flight**. Your Taker convinces you that your spouse is not worth the effort, and that you should engage in emotional divorce.

> **State of Withdrawal**
>
> The state of mind dominated by your Taker, which encourages you to emotionally withdraw from your spouse, neither giving nor taking.

In the state of withdrawal, you no longer feel emotionally bonded to each other or in love, and emotional defenses are raised. Neither of you wants to try to meet the other's needs, and both of you have given up on attempts to get your own needs met by the other. One becomes two. You are completely independent, united only in living arrangements, finances, and child rearing, although you may keep up appearances for neighbors and friends.

When one of you enters the state of withdrawal, the other usually follows. After all, what is the point? If she is meeting none of his needs and rebuffing every effort he makes to meet hers, he might as well give up too. The thoughtless behavior by each of you toward the other becomes too great to bear, so you stop caring. Trust is a faint memory.

Emotional needs can be met only when you allow them to be met. But when you are in the state of withdrawal, you don't want your spouse to meet your needs and you raise emotional defenses to prevent it from happening. Even if your spouse tries to meet an emotional need, your defensive wall blunts the effect and prevents any Love Bank deposits.

> **Emotional needs can be met only when you allow them to be met.**

Couples in withdrawal are in a state of emotional divorce. When they've been in withdrawal for a length of time, they sleep in separate rooms, take separate vacations, and eat meals at different times. They do not communicate unless they must. If that doesn't work, they either separate or obtain a legal divorce.

I've already explained that the states of intimacy and conflict discourage negotiating. In the state of withdrawal, spouses do not have the slightest interest in negotiating. In intimacy, spouses receive as soon as they ask. In conflict, they fight to try to get what they want. But in withdrawal, there is no discussion, no bargaining, not even arguing. In that state, spouses are unwilling to do anything for each other.

When a couple is in the state of withdrawal, the marriage seems hopeless. There is no willingness to be thoughtful or to meet each other's emotional needs and no willingness to even talk about the problems. It really is hopeless because neither spouse is at all interested in saving the marriage.

But the state of withdrawal doesn't usually last very long. Sooner than most couples think, at least one spouse has the presence of mind to try to break the deadlock. When that happens, it's possible for that spouse to lead the other all the way back to the state of intimacy. But it's possible only if the influence of the Giver and Taker is carefully controlled.

Getting Back to Intimacy

I have described the three states of mind in marriage as if you and your spouse experience them simultaneously. And many times, that's precisely what happens. But in some situations, you may find yourselves in different states of mind. One of you may disrupt the other's state of intimacy by being unable to meet an emotional need or by inadvertent thoughtlessness. Now in the state of conflict, the one that's offended begins to complain and nag and may even try to start a fight. As the complaints escalate, the one who was still in the state of intimacy is dragged into the state of conflict as well, and then the fighting begins in earnest.

If one of you uses his or her intelligence at any point along the way, you may lead the other on the road back from withdrawal to conflict and eventually back to intimacy.

Typically, if you fail in your efforts to resolve the conflict and if the unpleasant demands, disrespect, and anger escalate, one of you will go into withdrawal first and raise his or her emotional barriers. The one who remains in the state of conflict continues to argue, while the one who has withdrawn tries to escape. If the arguing spouse persists, the withdrawn spouse may be goaded to reenter the conflict state and fight back. Or the arguing spouse may give up and enter the withdrawal state too.

While the Taker is relentless in driving both of you into withdrawal, if one of you uses his or her intelligence at any point along the way, you may lead the other on the road back from withdrawal to conflict and eventually back to intimacy.

In withdrawal, you may intelligently decide to make a new effort to restore intimacy and toss out an olive branch. Your effort goes against the advice of your Taker, but you decide, correctly, that your Taker is leading you astray. Your Taker may partially go along with your plan and place you back into conflict, while your spouse is still in withdrawal. But now your Taker's advice is to make demands, show disrespect, and become angry, behavior that will not draw your spouse out of withdrawal but keep him or her there. Again you use your intelligence and ignore your Taker's advice.

Suppose your effort is an encouragement to your spouse and he or she eventually joins you in the state of conflict. Now you are both willing to have your needs met by the other, but both of your Takers are encouraging you to fight about it, rather than negotiate intelligently and peacefully. The intelligent thing for both of you to do is ignore the advice of the Taker. Even if only one of you is successful in avoiding the Taker's temptation to fight, you both have a chance to return to the state of intimacy. It takes two to argue, so if one of you makes an effort to avoid making demands and judgmental statements and tries to be thoughtful and meet the other's needs, the other spouse will usually calm down.

Once one of you sees the other's caring efforts and experiences Love Bank deposits, he or she will usually reenter the state of intimacy. But there's an irony that trips up some couples. Which spouse do you think is the first to experience the state of intimacy— the one who makes the first effort to meet the other's needs, or the recipient of that effort? You may have guessed it. The recipient of care is usually the first to return to the state of intimacy, and not the one who makes the greatest effort to save the relationship.

You cannot simply choose your state of mind.

You cannot simply choose your state of mind. It is usually determined by the way your spouse treats you and the way your emotions react to your situation. But you can use your intelligence to override the instincts that dominate your state of mind. If you make the effort to meet your spouse's needs first, your own needs will be met last. That's why the one who does the most to save a marriage is likely to be the last to experience the state of intimacy.

Your Taker will not be pleased with this arrangement, of course, and may try to sabotage it. You will need to make a deliberate and patient effort to override the Taker's instinct to retreat back to fighting and name-calling. But if you resist the instinct to argue, and instead focus attention on behaving thoughtfully and meeting your spouse's needs, your spouse will be encouraged to reciprocate, once he or she returns to the state of intimacy.

When your Love Bank balances are finally restored and your love for each other is triggered again, the struggle is over. You will have returned to intimacy, and in that state, everything you need to do for each other will seem almost effortless.

Pulling Together Makes Recovery Much Easier

The passage from intimacy through conflict to withdrawal is a slippery slope. You can get there before you know it, but it takes quite a bit of work to climb back up that hill.

While one of you can help by pulling the other back up, it's a lot easier when you both work together. And the best way to work back to intimacy from withdrawal and conflict is for both of you to use your intelligence.

In the above scenario, I have suggested that one of you can lift the other from one state of mind to the next. It can be done, but ideally you both should carry your own weight. And that happens when you both use your intelligence to make thoughtful decisions and meet each other's emotional needs. Regardless of the state of mind you happen to be in, you can override your emotional instincts to make intelligent decisions. That will not only speed up the movement from withdrawal and conflict back to intimacy, but it will help keep you in the state of intimacy much longer.

> Regardless of the state of mind you happen to be in, you can override your emotional instincts to make intelligent decisions.

I have made it sound as if your intelligence is only useful in the states of conflict and withdrawal, but it also comes in handy in the state of intimacy. Remember how most couples fall out of intimacy? They fail to negotiate fairly with each other. Their Giver sets them up for failure by being all too willing to sacrifice. So you need to use your intelligence to negotiate fairly even when you are in the state of intimacy.

Be intelligent about the way you resolve all of your conflicts. I have a rule for you to follow that will put your intelligence in charge permanently. Don't get me wrong, your Giver and Taker are useful advisors, but neither should dominate your decision making. You should use your intelligence, not your emotions, to make marital decisions, and this rule will guarantee the best outcome for you. It will help you negotiate when all of your instincts tell you either to give or to take, but not both. If you use this rule to resolve your marital conflicts, you will change from a negotiating idiot into a negotiating genius. I call it the Policy of Joint Agreement.

Key Principles

- Intimacy is a state of mind dominated by your Giver, who encourages you to give unconditionally to your spouse.
- Conflict is a state of mind dominated by your Taker, who encourages you to take unconditionally from your spouse.
- Withdrawal is a state of mind dominated by your Taker, who encourages you to withdraw emotionally from your spouse, neither giving nor taking.
- Regardless of which state spouses are in, negotiations can be very difficult, because in each case, emotional reactions tend to override intelligence.
- If one or, better yet, both spouses use their intelligence to resolve conflicts, rather than using their emotional reactions, they can climb from withdrawal to intimacy and stay there.

Thinking It Through

1. How does the state of intimacy affect your thinking and problem-solving strategies? Have you noticed that you tend to be unconditionally *caring* when you are in that state of mind? Think of conversations you have had with each other when in the state of intimacy. Were they conversations you would like to have more often?

2. How does the state of conflict affect your thinking and problem-solving strategies? Have you noticed that you tend to be unconditionally *selfish* when you are in that state of mind? Try to recall recent

conversations you have had with each other when in the state of conflict. Were they conversations you would like to avoid?

3. How does the state of withdrawal affect your thinking and problem-solving strategies? Have you noticed that you tend to avoid issues that have come between you when you are in that state of mind? Have you noticed how difficult it is to communicate about the simplest things?

4. Do one or both of you try to lead the other out of the state of withdrawal? If so, how do you do it? What works the best for each of you?

5. The next chapter will help you avoid the states of conflict and withdrawal, and if you find yourselves in them, it will help you lead each other out. Are you ready to learn how to do that?

chapter sixteen

THE POLICY OF JOINT AGREEMENT

Now that you have learned about your Giver and Taker, and how they create three states of mind that just about doom any effort to negotiate in marriage, you should be ready to hear my solution to the problem. Quite frankly, it wouldn't make much sense to you without the background I have just provided. But if you agree with me that your instincts tend to make fair marital negotiation almost impossible, the rule I suggest should make perfect sense to you. And I hope you and your spouse use this rule for the rest of your lives together.

When in the state of intimacy, your Giver encourages you to make *your spouse* happy and avoid doing anything to hurt your spouse. In the state of conflict, your Taker encourages you to make *you* happy, and avoid doing anything to hurt *you*. Both of these objectives are important because they represent care for both you and your spouse. Both your Giver and your Taker give you good advice, and I wanted my rule to support it.

But the rule also had to avoid the worst advice of your Giver and Taker. In the state of intimacy, your Giver encourages you to *sacrifice your own happiness* so that your spouse can be happy. In the state of conflict, your Taker encourages you to *let your spouse sacrifice* so that you can be happy. Neither of these is a good idea because in both cases someone gets hurt.

In marriage your interests and your spouse's interests should be considered simultaneously. One of you should not suffer, even willingly, for the benefit of the other, because when either of you suffers, one is gaining at the other's expense. And if you both care about each other, you will not let that happen. When either of you is willing to let the other sacrifice for you, you are momentarily lapsing into a state of selfishness that must somehow be corrected before damage is done. I needed a rule to provide that correction.

I must warn you that when you read this rule for the first time, you may think I'm crazy to be suggesting such a thing. But the more you think about it and the more you follow it in your marriage, you will recognize it as the breakthrough you need in the marital logjam created by your Giver and Taker. It will give your intelligence an opportunity to resolve your conflicts instead of turning them over to your emotions.

The Policy of Joint Agreement
Never do anything without an enthusiastic agreement between you and your spouse.

After carefully examining this policy, you will probably have two contrasting reactions: If both you and your spouse follow this agreement, your Giver will like the part that requires your spouse's enthusiastic agreement before you do anything, while your Taker will like the way it requires your enthusiastic agreement before your spouse does anything. On the other hand, your Giver will think you are being selfish when you don't do whatever it takes to make your spouse happy (even if that means doing something you don't "enthusiastically" agree with), and your Taker will think you are just plain dumb to let your spouse's lack of enthusiasm prevent you from doing whatever makes

> If you follow the Policy of Joint Agreement, it will prevent you from giving so much that it hurts you or taking so much that you hurt your spouse.

you happy. Yet, if you follow this rule, it will prevent you from giving so much that it hurts you or taking so much that you hurt your spouse.

Becoming Thoughtful through the Policy of Joint Agreement

The Policy of Joint Agreement will help you become sensitive to each other's feelings especially when you do not feel like being sensitive. Since the policy requires you to have each other's enthusiastic agreement before you do anything, it forces you to ask each other a very important question, "How do you feel about what I would like to do?" That simple question and its answer are the next best thing to empathy. You may not actually feel what your spouse feels, but at least you give your spouse the opportunity to tell you how he or she feels. And then, even if you find yourself in a thoughtless mood, the Policy of Joint Agreement prevents you from doing anything thoughtless.

> Compatibility is building a way of life that is comfortable for both spouses.

You are now a team, not two disinterested individuals. You should work together to achieve objectives that benefit both of you simultaneously. It just makes good sense. Why should one of you consider your own interests so important that you can run roughshod over the interests of the other? That's a formula for marital disaster, and yet you may have been making this mistake from your honeymoon on.

When I first see a couple in marital crisis, each of them is usually living his or her life as if the other hardly exists. They make thoughtless decisions regularly because often they don't care how the other feels. As a result, when I introduce the Policy of Joint Agreement to them, they find it totally irrational. They have developed so many inconsiderate habits that the policy seems to threaten their entire way of life.

At first, the policy seems impossible to follow because they do not want to abandon their thoughtless and insensitive habits and activities. But once they start to follow the policy, it becomes easier and easier to come to an agreement, as they replace their thoughtless habits with those that take each other's feelings into account.

That's what compatibility is all about—building a way of life that is comfortable for both spouses. When they create a lifestyle that they both enjoy and appreciate, they build compatibility into their marriage.

Negotiating with the Policy of Joint Agreement

The Policy of Joint Agreement prevents either of you from making unilateral decisions about anything, so you must discuss every decision you make before action can be taken. Once the question "How do you feel about what I would like to do?" is asked and your spouse's reaction is not enthusiastic, you have the choice of either abandoning the entire idea or trying to discover alternative ways of making it possible.

> **With the goal of enthusiastic agreement, you will be forced to abandon the thoughtless and abusive strategies of your Taker.**

And that's where negotiation begins. With practice, you can both become experts at getting what you need in ways that can have mutual and enthusiastic agreement. Once you agree to this policy and get into the habit of using it to make your decisions, fair negotiation will become a way of life for you.

With the goal of enthusiastic agreement, you will be forced to abandon the thoughtless and abusive strategies of your Taker. Demands are out of the question, because they do not engender enthusiastic agreement—demands force one of you to lose so that the other can win. The same can be said for disrespectful judgments and angry outbursts. What role do any of those Love Busters have in a discussion where the goal is enthusiastic agreement? In their place, you will learn to make requests and express opinions, while showing respect for the opinions of your spouse. The

ACTION STEP

Use the Policy of Joint Agreement to negotiate fairly.

sheer foolishness of demands, disrespect, and anger are evident when a mutually enthusiastic agreement is your goal.

Why *Enthusiastic* Agreement?

The word *enthusiastic* should get your attention. It's a Taker's word because your Taker will be enthusiastic about an agreement that's in your own best interest. And your spouse's Taker will be enthusiastic about things in his or her best interest.

Givers never show much enthusiasm, although they are willing to help sacrificially when needed. Givers will agree to almost anything, but not enthusiastically.

Since your agreements must be good for both of you, the only way to know that your Takers have given them the stamp of approval is to look for mutual enthusiasm. If it's not there, you both should keep searching for better alternatives.

How does this policy work out in real life? Let's consider three alternatives to the Policy of Joint Agreement.

Couple A: Tom and Mary do not discuss their plans with each other, much less agree. They just go ahead and plan their days with no consideration whatsoever for each other's feelings. If Tom wants to stop for a drink on the way home from work, he does, without asking Mary how she would feel about it. She never knows when he'll be home. If she wants to go shopping after he comes home from work, she says good-bye to the kids and out the door she goes, hardly noticing Tom, let alone asking him if he'd watch their children.

Tom and Mary have adopted a strategy common among those in the state of withdrawal. I'm sure you recognize it as the Taker's strategy. They have become terribly incompatible; each has developed a lifestyle and personal habits that ignore the other's feelings. When they argue, it's about who spends the money or who watches the children. They are headed for divorce.

Couple B: Rick and Janet use a somewhat better decision-making strategy. They discuss their plans with each other and think about how they would affect the other, but they both reserve the right to make the final decision, and each of them occasionally does things that the other doesn't like.

For instance, there is an optional business trip that Rick could take, but it coincides with Janet's birthday. He talks it over with her, listens to her wishes, but decides to go anyway. Janet is offered a community leadership position that will take her away from home several nights a week. Rick explains how it would complicate his life, but she accepts the offer. To the extent that they disregard each other's feelings, they are building an incompatible lifestyle.

This couple is often in the state of conflict, because once in a while their decision-making strategy causes one to gain at the other's expense. Discussing their plans helps them understand each other, and they often accommodate each other with that understanding. For example, when Rick learned that Janet objected to a certain aftershave lotion that he bought, he stopped using it. But because their thoughtfulness is not consistent, their feelings are often hurt, and that arouses their Takers, plunging them into conflict quite often, and even into withdrawal once in a while.

Couple C: Dan and Carla go one step further: They do not go ahead with most decisions unless there is agreement. But they are willing to accept **reluctant** agreement. Their Givers make a valiant effort to override the concerns of their Takers, and even though their hearts are in the right place, their unselfish approach actually encourages some incompatibility.

One Monday night, Dan wanted to watch football with one of his friends and invited Carla to go with him. She not only refused to go with him but let him know that she didn't even want him to go. He reluctantly agreed to stay at home that evening but he resented her for ruining what could have been fun. All night he was quiet, thinking about the game. By the time they went to bed, Carla wished she had let him go because he was so unpleasant to be around.

Dan's intelligence was strong enough to override his Taker's wishes to watch football, but not strong enough to keep his Taker from vigorously protesting. Dan got (and delivered) his Taker's message loud and clear. Before the evening was over, he flew into a rage over some little thing. Three days later when he was telling me about the incident, he had forgotten what had made him lose his temper, but he sure remembered having given up *Monday Night Football*.

Reluctant agreement *seems* like a satisfactory solution to many couples. Most of us view personal sacrifice as a noble thing—giving up our well-being for the good of others—but it's really very risky in a marital relationship. When you reluctantly agree to some course of action with your spouse, it means that he or she is gaining at your expense. And that can tip the delicate balance of your marriage. If a decision is not in the interest of both of you, it is not in the best interest of your relationship.

> If a decision is not in the interest of both of you, it is not in the best interest of your relationship.

That's not to say you should never sacrifice. We have all sacrificed our own short-term interests for a long-term interest. Not every decision we make can, or should, be viewed as benefiting us immediately. For example, I went through quite a bit of self-sacrifice when I earned a Ph.D. in psychology. It was no fun, I assure you. Yet my Taker was with me in this plan because it could see future value in my decision.

The same is true in my relationship with my wife, Joyce. I am willing to sacrifice my immediate pleasure for something that will give us both long-term pleasure. Having children fits into that category. I knew that Joyce and I would have to work harder after Jennifer and Steve were born. Still, my Taker (like Joyce's) was enthusiastic about the future fulfillment involved in having children.

What I'm saying is that your Taker can be enthusiastic about sacrifice, if it's in your long-term interest. When you agree to something reluctantly, however, you are sacrificing your own best interest even though you see no long-term benefits. That's why reluctant agreement usually gets sabotaged later by your Taker. When the time comes to follow through on a reluctant agreement, don't be surprised if your Taker pulls the plug on it at the last minute.

So let's evaluate the three alternatives to the Policy of Joint Agreement illustrated in couples A, B, and C. I think we would all agree that Tom and Mary, our first couple, are in deep trouble as they pass each other like ships in the night. Their strategy of self-centered decision making doesn't work in marriage, and couples that follow it usually divorce.

Rick and Janet, couple B, have taken a step in the right direction, but they're in trouble too. They still allow thoughtlessness to come between them, robbing them of the intimacy that they need in marriage.

Most of us can best relate to our third couple, Dan and Carla, with their reluctant agreement. You can probably think of many sacrifices you've made to accommodate your spouse. (Incidentally, although your spouse has probably made just as many sacrifices for you, I'll bet you can't think of nearly as many examples of his or her reluctant agreement to accommodate you.)

Dan and Carla's marriage will survive, but their habit of reluctant agreement will allow stubborn pockets of incompatibility to remain. Their Takers will feel left out and will occasionally cause a ruckus. It's only when they take the final step, when they continue to negotiate about every conflict until there's an **enthusiastic** agreement between them, that marital compatibility flourishes. Then they create a lifestyle that benefits both of them simultaneously. When that happens, it can truly be said that they live in harmony with each other.

> **Couples that follow the Policy of Joint Agreement and meet each other's most important emotional needs fall in love and stay in love with each other.**

When you adopt the Policy of Joint Agreement, it will help insulate you from many of the destructive forces that ruin marriages. And it will help you learn to meet each other's most important emotional needs in ways that are mutually fulfilling and enjoyable. Couples that follow this policy and meet each other's most important emotional needs fall in love and stay in love with each other. That's the most powerful incentive of all for following the policy.

The First Step in Negotiation

As soon as you and your spouse adopt the Policy of Joint Agreement as your guide in marriage, you will have taken a giant step forward in your ability to negotiate. That's because you will be forced to ask each other the question "How do you feel about what I would like to do?" Prior to your consideration of this policy, that question may never have come up. You would make your decisions unilaterally, without any consideration for each other's feelings. But the Policy of Joint Agreement *forces* you to be considerate, especially when you don't feel like it. When you ask the question "How do you feel about what I would like to do?" you take the first steps in negotiation—raising the issue and seeking an agreement before any action is taken.

> **The Policy of Joint Agreement forces you to be considerate, especially when you don't feel like it.**

Your Giver doesn't care how you feel about your spouse's behavior, as long as your spouse is having fun doing it. And your Taker doesn't care about how your spouse feels about your behavior, as long as you do it without your spouse's interference. So this question "How do you feel?" is completely foreign to the way either your Giver or your Taker approach a problem. At first, the question will seem very strange to you, even humorous. That's because your instincts don't think in those terms, and that's precisely why marital negotiation is so tough. Yet that question is at the very core of every negotiation, and you must force yourselves to ask it until it becomes a habit.

While the question, "How would you feel?" gets negotiation started, and the Policy of Joint Agreement is your final goal (enthusiastic agreement), you may not be entirely familiar with what should go on in between. In other words, how do you arrive at an enthusiastic agreement?

I have devoted the rest of this book to helping you learn to agree enthusiastically. In the next chapter, I will explain a step-by-step procedure that I suggest you follow whenever you negotiate. And then, in the last chapter, I will give you a few illustrations of how this procedure is carried out.

Dan and Carla (couple C) needed an effective negotiating procedure when the *Monday Night Football* issue came up. Dan wanted to go out to watch TV with his friends and wanted Carla to join him. But Carla wanted him to stay home with her. Because they were not used to negotiating with each other, they did not come up with any other alternatives from which they could choose. So, regardless of their decision, one of them would end up feeling resentful. The goal of fair negotiation is to arrive at a decision that they both can agree to enthusiastically, but Dan and Carla had no experience with such negotiating because they had settled for reluctant agreement.

> If you keep practicing, eventually you will reach wise decisions with very little effort.

If you are like Dan and Carla and have not been in the habit of negotiating an enthusiastic agreement, I suggest you begin formally and practice the steps that I suggest. That way, even though it may be slow and awkward for you at first, at least you will be making decisions that meet the conditions of the Policy of Joint Agreement. When you and your spouse eventually become comfortable negotiating with each other, it won't seem so formal to you. In fact most of the time you will be negotiating on the run, taking as little as a few minutes to come to an enthusiastic agreement. If you keep practicing, eventually you will reach wise decisions with very little effort.

Key Principles

- The Policy of Joint Agreement—Never do anything without an enthusiastic agreement between you and your spouse—will prevent you from giving so much it hurts you or taking so much it hurts your spouse.

- The Policy of Joint Agreement prevents you from being thoughtless, even if you're in a thoughtless mood.

- Replacing thoughtless habits with those that take each other's feelings into account builds compatibility into your marriage.

- With the Policy of Joint Agreement you and your spouse will learn to negotiate so that you both enthusiastically agree with every decision you make.

- Mutual enthusiasm for an agreement is essential so that both you and your spouse will be committed to it. If you aren't both enthusiastic about a decision, you need to search for a better alternative.

Thinking It Through

1. What are the advantages and disadvantages of asking each other the question, *How do you feel about what I would like to do?* One advantage is that it helps you develop empathy for each other. If you cannot actually feel what your spouse feels, the next best thing is to ask how your spouse feels. Do you agree with me that the question, *How do you feel about what I would like to do?* helps you understand how you affect each other?

2. If you have not already guessed it, one disadvantage to the question, *How would you feel . . . ?* is that it can expose your thoughtlessness. If you go ahead and do something that your spouse just told you would hurt him or her, you've blown the illusion that you are willing to consider your spouse's feelings when you make a decision. This is the Taker at work. Have either of you ever avoided asking each other about what you were planning because you knew you were going to do it anyway?

3. The answer to the question, *How would you feel . . . ?* provides valuable information about how you affect each other before you actually do anything. And then the Policy of Joint Agreement injects fairness into the way you try to resolve conflicts when the plans of one of you will hurt the other.

   The main purpose of the Policy of Joint Agreement is to force you to negotiate with each other, instead of making unilateral decisions. In fact, without the Policy of Joint Agreement, you may find yourselves with very little will to negotiate. Think of a few examples of recent decisions that either of you made unilaterally, and think of ways you could have made a better decision if you had been forced to use the Policy of Joint Agreement.

4. Discuss the pros and cons of doing nothing until you have reached an agreement. What are some obvious exceptions to the Policy of Joint Agreement (for example, a life-and-death emergency when there is no time to discuss alternatives)? When is the Policy of Joint Agreement most appropriately applied?

My primary reason for advocating this policy is that the decisions often become lifestyle habits. It's important that the Policy of Joint Agreement determine your habits and repeated activities because they have the greatest effect on your Love Bank balances.

5. How do you feel about "enthusiastic agreement," as opposed to "reluctant agreement"?

Discuss the ways couples A, B, and C resolved conflicts. Which of them most closely characterizes the way you have been making decisions? Or have you already been following the Policy of Joint Agreement?

chapter seventeen

FOUR GUIDELINES FOR
SUCCESSFUL
NEGOTIATION

Let's begin with the assumption that you and your spouse do not agree about something. It may be about how to meet an unmet need or about overcoming a thoughtless habit that is bothering one of you. In fact it can be about anything that has become a conflict.

Chances are that you have been responding to this issue in one of three ways: (1) ignoring your own feelings and doing it your spouse's way, (2) ignoring your spouse's feelings and doing it your way, or (3) ignoring the problem entirely. Negotiation, however, requires something very different—taking your feelings and the feelings of your spouse into account simultaneously. The following guidelines will help you achieve that very important objective.

Guideline 1

Set ground rules to make negotiation pleasant and safe. Most couples view negotiation as a trip to the torture chamber. That's because their efforts are usually fruitless, and they come away from the

ACTION STEP

Identify an issue that you and your spouse cannot agree on enthusiastically.

175

ACTION STEP

Set ground rules for negotiation.

experience battered and bruised. Who wants to negotiate when you have nothing but disappointment and pain to look forward to?

So before you begin to negotiate, set some basic ground rules to make sure that you both enjoy the experience. Why? Because you repeat activities that you like and avoid those you don't like. Since you should negotiate as often as a conflict arises, it should always be an enjoyable experience so you make it a regular part of your married life.

To be certain that you will have a pleasant and safe negotiating environment, I suggest three ground rules:

Ground Rule 1: *Try to be pleasant and cheerful throughout negotiations.* It's fairly easy to start discussing an issue while in a good mood. But negotiations can open a can of worms, so be prepared for negative emotional reactions. Your spouse may begin to feel uncomfortable about something you say. In fact, out of the clear blue, he or she may inform you that there will be no further discussion.

I know how upset and defensive couples can become when they first discover they don't agree with each other. That's why I first coach them individually to prepare them for negative comments. I simply tell them what I am telling you: Try to be as positive and cheerful as you can be, especially if your spouse says something that offends you.

Ground Rule 2: *Put safety first. Do not make demands, show disrespect, or become angry when you negotiate, even if your spouse makes demands, shows disrespect, or becomes angry with you.* Once you have told each other what is bothering you or what you want, you have entered one of the most dangerous phases of negotiation. If your feelings have been hurt, you are tempted to retaliate. Your Taker is very persuasive at this point, and unless you make a special effort to resist its advice, your negotiation will turn into an argument. If you can keep each other safe, you will be able to use your intelligence to help you make the changes you both need.

Ground Rule 3: *If you reach an impasse and you do not seem to be getting anywhere or if one of you is starting to make demands, show disrespect, or become angry, stop negotiating and come back to the issue later.* Just because you can't resolve a problem at a particular point in time doesn't mean you can't find an intelligent solution in the future. Don't let an impasse prevent you from giving yourself a chance to think about the issue. Let it incubate for a while, and you'll be amazed what your mind can do.

> Just because you can't resolve a problem at a particular point in time doesn't mean you can't find an intelligent solution in the future.

If your negotiation turns sour and one of you succumbs to the temptation of the Taker with demands, disrespect, or anger, end the discussion by changing the subject to something more pleasant. After a brief pause, your spouse may apologize and wish to return to the subject that was so upsetting. But don't go back into the minefield until it has been swept clear of mines. The mines, of course, are demands, disrespect, and anger, and you must discuss how to avoid them before you return to the issue. You can't negotiate if your Takers' destructive instincts control your discussion.

Guideline 2

Identify the problem from both perspectives. Once you have set ground rules that guarantee a safe and enjoyable discussion, you are ready to negotiate. But where do you begin? First, you must understand the problem both from your perspective and from that of your spouse.

Most couples go into marital negotiation without doing their homework. They don't fully understand the conflict itself nor do they understand each other's perspective. In many cases, they are not even sure what they really want.

One of the responsibilities of a marriage counselor is to help couples clarify the issues that sep-

ACTION STEP

Identify the problem from both perspectives.

arate them. I'm amazed at how often the clarification itself solves the problem. "Oh, that's what we've been fighting about!" many couples say. And once they understand the issue and each other's opinions, they realize that the conflict is not as serious as they thought. Or when the issue is clarified, the solution is immediately apparent and the conflict is resolved.

Respect is the key to success in this phase of negotiation. Once the issue has been identified and you hear each other's perspectives, it is extremely important to understand each other instead of trying to straighten each other out. Remember that your goal is **enthusiastic** agreement, and there is no way you will be enthusiastic if you reject each other's perspective. In fact the only way you will reach an enthusiastic agreement is if you not only understand each other but also come up with a solution that accommodates each other's perspective.

> **Respect is the key to success in the initial phase of negotiation.**

It's so much easier to negotiate the right way when your goal is enthusiastic agreement. It eliminates all the strategies that attempt to wear each other down with abuse. You may as well forget about demands because they never lead to an enthusiastic agreement. The same can be said for disrespectful judgments and angry outbursts. If you are looking for real solutions to your problem, you will find them in whatever yields an enthusiastic agreement.

But when I take demands, disrespect, and anger away from some couples, they are left feeling naked. They don't know how to discuss an issue if they can't demand, show disrespect, or express their anger. And without those Love Busters they often feel hopeless about resolving their problems, because they have rarely approached their problems with the goal of finding a win-win solution. They simply don't know how to do it. It's as if the only way they know how to communicate in marriage is through demands, disrespect, and anger.

Is that true of you and your spouse? If so, remember that with practice you will begin to feel more comfortable approaching every conflict with the goal of mutual agreement. You learn to ask each other questions, not to embarrass each other but to gain a fuller understanding of what it would take to make each other happy. And when you think you have the information you need to consider win-win solutions, you are ready for the next step.

Guideline 3

Brainstorm with abandon. You've set the ground rules. You've identified the problem from each other's perspective. Now you're ready for the creative part—looking for solutions that you think will make you both happy. I know that can seem impossible if you and your spouse have drifted into incompatibility. But the climb back to intimacy has to start somewhere, and if you put your minds to it, you'll think of options that please you both.

The secret to understanding your spouse is to think like your spouse's Taker. It's easy to appeal to your spouse's Giver. "If she really loves me, she'll let me do this," or "He'll be thoughtful enough to agree with that, I'm sure." But lasting peace must be forged with your spouse's Taker, so your solutions must appeal to your spouse's most selfish instincts. At the same time, they must also appeal to your own selfish instincts.

When you brainstorm, quantity is often more important than quality. Let your minds run wild; go with just about any thought that might satisfy both of your Takers. If you let your creative side run free, you are more likely to find a lasting solution.

Carry a pad of paper or a pocket notebook with you so you can write down ideas as you think of them throughout the day. Some problems may require days of thought and pages of ideas. But keep in mind your goal—a solution that would appeal to both of your Takers.

Resist one type of solution that your Giver and Taker may suggest—the "I'll-let-you-do-what-you-want-this-time-if-you-let-me-do-what-I-want-next-time" solution. For example, imagine that you want to go out with your friends after work, leaving your spouse with the children. So to arrive at an enthusiastic agreement for that thoughtless activ-

ACTION STEP

Brainstorm with abandon.

ity, you suggest that you take the children another night so that your spouse can go out with his or her friends.

What you're really proposing here is that each of you will sacrifice so that the other can have fun. The problem with that arrangement is that you are agreeing to behavior that makes one of you unhappy whenever the other is happy, and as I've said earlier, once you have made an agreement, it can easily turn into a habit.

> **When you brainstorm, quantity is often more important than quality.**

The Giver and Taker suggest those win-lose solutions because they don't understand win-win solutions. Their concept of fairness is that if you are both suffering equally, that's fair. My view of negotiation is that by the time you are finished, you have arrived at a solution that causes neither of you to suffer. And each part of the solution should not require either of you to sacrifice so that the other can be happy.

Guideline 4

Choose the solution that meets the conditions of the Policy of Joint Agreement—mutual and enthusiastic agreement. After brainstorming, you will have come up with some good and some bad solutions. Now you need to sort through them. Good solutions are those both you and your spouse consider desirable. In other words they meet the conditions of the Policy of Joint Agreement. Bad solutions, on the other hand, take the feelings of only one spouse into account—at the expense of the other. The best solution is the one that makes you and your spouse most enthusiastic.

ACTION STEP

Choose a solution on which you both enthusiastically agree.

Many problems are relatively easy to solve. You will be amazed at how quickly you can find an enthusiastic agreement to some problems when you have decided to hold off on any action until you both agree. That's because when you know you must take each other's feelings into account, you become increasingly aware of what it will take to reach a mutual agreement. Instead of considering options that are clearly not in your spouse's best interest, you reject them immediately and begin to think of options you know would make both you and your spouse happy. It's amazing how smart you can be when you direct your mind to find smart solutions.

For example, consider the situation we mentioned above. You would like to go out with your friends after work, leaving your spouse with the children. Before you had agreed to the Policy of Joint Agreement, you may have simply called your spouse to say you would be late, or worse yet, arrived home late without having called. But now you must come to an enthusiastic agreement prior to the event. It certainly restricts your freedom of choice but, on the other hand, it protects your spouse from your thoughtless behavior.

After having presented your case, you would probably hear immediate objections. Your spouse might not appreciate your having fun while he or she is home battling the kids. "Besides," your spouse might mention, "our leisure activities should be with each other." In response, you might suggest that your spouse drop the kids off at your parents' (whom you will call to make the arrangements) and join you.

If you and your spouse can enthusiastically agree on that suggestion, you are home free. Your parents take your children for a couple of hours, and your spouse joins you wherever it is you were planning to meet your friends. Problem solved. In fact, if going out after work with friends becomes a regular event, you can plan ahead for it by arranging the child care in advance.

Of course, other problems can be more difficult to solve, involving many steps. Learning how to meet each other's emotional needs, for example, can require quite a bit of trial and error, along with the time and energy it takes to create the habits that eventually make meeting a need almost effortless.

If one of you struggles with an addiction, you will find that the Policy of Joint Agreement simply cannot be followed at all until you have overcome the addiction. Whether it's drugs, alcohol, sex, gambling, or any other addiction, you will find that thoughtfulness is almost impossible to practice as long as you are addicted.

You must sweep the addiction completely out of your life before you will be able to negotiate in the way I have suggested.

When a couple has tried to follow my advice but can't seem to negotiate with each other regardless of how hard they try, addiction is usually the culprit. In fact a good way to determine if you are addicted to a substance or activity is to see if you can follow the Policy of Joint Agreement after you have agreed to it. If you find you can't, chances are you're an addict.

If you follow the guidelines I have suggested, negotiation can be an enjoyable way to learn about each other. And if you avoid unpleasant scenes and negotiate to an enthusiastic agreement, you can resolve with relative ease all of the many conflicts you will have throughout life.

> **Negotiation can be an enjoyable way to learn about each other.**

One last point: Whenever a conflict arises, keep in mind the importance of depositing as many love units as possible while avoiding withdrawals. In other words, use the opportunity to find a solution that will make your spouse happy and avoid solutions that make either of you unhappy. And make sure that the way you find that solution also deposits love units and avoids withdrawals.

I've given you some pretty straightforward principles in this chapter, but you may still wonder about how all of this really works in practice. So in the last chapter I'll give you a few examples that may help you learn to negotiate skillfully. As you read them, you may even find some good ideas for resolving the conflicts in your marriage, because the illustrations I chose are very common.

Follow Through

Step 1: Discuss the pros and cons of the Policy of Joint Agreement. You will tend to want your spouse to consider your feelings when he or she makes a decision, but you may not be quite as willing to consider your spouse's feelings when you make a decision. It's the Taker at work. Discuss how the Policy of Joint

Agreement injects fairness into the way you try to resolve conflicts.

Step 2:   The main purpose of the Policy of Joint Agreement is to force you to negotiate with each other, instead of making unilateral decisions. In fact, without the Policy of Joint Agreement, you may find yourselves with very little will to negotiate. Think of a few examples of recent decisions that either of you made unilaterally and think of ways you could have made a better decision if you had been forced to use the Policy of Joint Agreement.

Step 3:   The Four Guidelines for Successful Negotiation sound like a very formal procedure to follow. But in practice, they can be implemented quickly if you are in the habit of using them. To help familiarize you with these guidelines, and how to use the Policy of Joint Agreement, I suggest the following exercise.

Go to a grocery store together, without your children, and for about fifteen minutes select items for your cart that you would both be enthusiastic about buying. This should be "pretend" buying, and is only to be used for practice. Your actual grocery purchases should be done the way you normally buy groceries. You don't need to actually buy any of the items in your cart when you are finished. I chose this exercise so you will have a chance to make decisions on an issue that has no real practical consequences for either of you. That way, you can avoid the emotional reactions that accompany real conflicts you may be having.

If one of you wants an item that the other cannot be enthusiastic about, negotiate with that spouse to try to create enthusiasm (demands, disrespect, and anger do not work, so don't even think of using them). You will find that the strategy of suggesting a test of the item to demonstrate its value to the reluctant spouse will often have favorable results. But avoid making bargains that let you have one item that your spouse doesn't like in exchange for your spouse having an item you don't like. Make sure that every item is either chosen with an enthusiastic agreement or doesn't go into the cart.

Repeat this exercise on several occasions until you can fill your cart with groceries in the 15 minutes you have scheduled. The very act of asking each other how you feel regarding each item in question, and holding off on making a decision until you have agreement, is an extremely important habit to learn if you want to become compatible and in love with each other. When you think you have gotten the hang of it, tackle some real conflicts you have been unable to resolve.

chapter eighteen

HOW TO RESOLVE EVERYDAY
PROBLEMS

If you haven't already figured it out, let me tell you that I think the Policy of Joint Agreement is the best thing since sliced bread. In one simple rule you have a way to solve almost every marital problem, which will help you fall in love and stay in love.

But you may need a little help getting the hang of how to use it when you and your spouse have a conflict. So in this chapter I'll present some common problems in marriage and show you how the Policy of Joint Agreement can solve them in a way that builds Love Bank balances. Then you'll be well on your way toward creating the love that you want to have for each other.

Resolving Conflicts over Friends and Relatives

Judy's Giver worked overtime. Whenever someone was in need, Judy rushed to the rescue. Bill was attracted to that trait when they were dating, especially when he was on the receiving end of her generosity. After marriage, though, it became a source of conflict when Judy's sister, Barbara, and Barbara's husband, Jack, moved in with them while Jack was "looking for work."

Bill didn't have any say in the matter. He came home one day to find his in-laws' possessions filling his house. That alone upset him, but it got worse as the weeks dragged on. Barbara and Jack seemed to be permanent fixtures.

"We cannot continue to support your sister and brother-in-law," Bill finally told Judy. "He'll just have to find a job like everyone else."

"But he's tried," Judy pleaded, "and if we don't help, who will? I can't just put my sister out on the street."

Our Giver can get us into a lot of trouble because it is willing to see us suffer for the sake of others. And when we're married, it's not just *our* Giver that we have to watch out for. Our spouse's Giver can also give us fits when it's generous at our expense. That's what Bill was up against. Judy's Giver wanted Bill to sacrifice along with Judy. When is it wrong to be generous? When your generosity takes advantage of your spouse. Judy was willing to suffer to help her sister survive but she made her husband suffer along with her.

When is it wrong to be generous? When your generosity takes advantage of your spouse.

As time went on, Bill became increasingly convinced that Judy cared more for her sister than for him. That belief was underscored by the fact that she was not able to meet his emotional needs the way she had in the past because they had lost much of their privacy. In addition, they were now supporting four people and were having trouble paying their bills.

Again and again Bill tried to get Judy to ask the in-laws to leave, but Judy insisted on letting them stay until Jack found a job. "I just can't turn my sister away. You'll have to be patient."

But Bill's patience ran out. So many love units had drained out of Judy's account that eventually there were none left. He had lost his love for Judy and he saw no purpose in being married to her, especially if it meant having to support his lazy in-laws as well. So he moved out.

Bill's decision brought Bill and Judy to my office for counseling. It didn't take long for Judy to realize that her generosity had been at Bill's expense, and she was willing to follow the Policy of Joint Agreement from that day on. She would never again make a decision without his enthusiastic agreement.

But Judy raised a very important issue. How should the Policy of Joint Agreement be applied to a decision that has already been made unilaterally? The damage is already done so why not see it through to the bitter end? She wanted her sister and brother-in-law to stay until he could find a job, and from then on she would follow the Policy of Joint Agreement.

Your friends and relatives can create problems in your marriage when their interests and the interests of your spouse are in conflict.

I explained to her that when the Policy of Joint Agreement has been violated, and a decision has been made without a joint agreement, a couple must correct the decision as quickly as possible. In this case it meant going back to her decision to invite Jack and Barbara to live with them and making that decision again, this time with the Policy of Joint Agreement in mind. Since she now knew that Bill would not agree to that arrangement, she had no choice but to ask her sister and brother-in-law to find another place to live. Even though Bill had lost his love for Judy, he agreed to give their marriage one more chance. As soon as Jack and Barbara moved out, Bill moved back in.

Now they could apply the Policy of Joint Agreement to their care of Judy's sister. And Bill was willing to help, as long as his interests were taken into account. Remarkably, he enthusiastically offered to loan Jack and Barbara enough money to pay rent for a few months and he even agreed to let them use some of the furniture they had used while living in his home. Bill and Judy were in enthusiastic agreement because they were not sacrificing anything they needed to be happy. And since they had enough privacy to meet each other's emotional needs, Bill's love for Judy returned within a few weeks.

From that one experience, which almost ruined their marriage, they learned to apply the Policy of Joint Agreement to all their decisions, and as far as I know, Judy's generosity never again got them into such serious marital trouble.

Your friends and relatives can create problems in your marriage when their interests and the interests of your spouse are in conflict. There are many situations where you cannot please your friends and family and please your spouse at the same time. In those situations the Policy of Joint Agreement protects your marriage from the common yet tragic mistake of pleasing your friends and family at your spouse's expense. It demonstrates your care and preserves the love you have for each other.

Resolving Conflicts over Child Discipline

Alex had a short fuse. His friends and family all knew it. But when he fell in love with Christine, he cared so much for her that he managed to keep his temper under control whenever he was with her. Christine became his bride because of his victory over this ugly Love Buster.

Their marriage went well because he kept his vow never to subject her to his angry outbursts. He never punished her either verbally or physically. However, he had been brought up in a tradition where heavy-handed discipline of children was considered the father's duty. When Alex was a child, his father had beaten him on many occasions. If he disobeyed, he could expect disastrous consequences, which he often experienced.

When Alex and Christine had their first child, Alex expected the same unwavering obedience that his parents had expected of him. Whenever little David misbehaved, Alex disciplined him the way *he* had been disciplined as a child.

The first time this happened, Christine became very upset and begged Alex to stop, but he continued using his violent methods whenever David misbehaved. Finally Christine went to her pastor for help. Recommending that she leave the discipline up to her husband, the pastor gave her examples of children who grew up to be criminals because women raised them without a father's punishment.

The pastor's advice did more harm than good. Alex had actually been holding back his temper somewhat because he realized how it affected Christine. But now that he had his pastor's permission to do whatever he felt was right regarding discipline, he released all his pent-up fury on young David. Whenever he felt irritated about something, he punished his son even more severely than before, and David was beginning to be very afraid of his dad.

All the while, Alex was careful never to treat Christine abusively. In fact he went out of his way to be sure she understood that his punishment of David was a father's responsibility, something that had to be done. But still she suffered every time he punished the child, crying as if he were punishing her. Even though Alex had shown her exceptional care in other ways, this punishment caused a huge withdrawal from her Love Bank.

What should Alex do? How would you try to solve this problem?

The answer should be obvious by now. If Alex and Christine were to agree to the Policy of Joint Agreement, he would never beat David again. Every act of discipline would have to be with Christine's enthusiastic agreement, and Alex would have to radically change his approach to discipline to obtain that agreement.

> **Every couple's joint methods of discipline are superior to their individual methods.**

In my experience counseling families, I have found that every couple's *joint* methods of discipline are superior to their *individual* methods. In other words, couples are wiser in the way they train their children when they agree on a training method. By discussing options and agreeing on a particular approach, they eliminate many of the foolish and impulsive acts of discipline that either one of them might try individually. Furthermore, children take parents more seriously when they both agree on discipline.

Christine wanted Alex to focus more attention on David's good behavior than on his bad behavior. She wanted him to reward his son far more often than he punished him. And she wanted the punishment to be nonviolent—taking away privileges rather than physical beatings or verbal assaults.

Deep down Alex knew she was right. He knew how resentful he was about the way he had been treated as a child, yet he had always assumed that it was somehow a father's responsibility to physically punish his children. But when he came to realize how much he had been hurting Christine whenever he punished David, he enthusiastically agreed to her plan. And the more he thought about it, the more he knew that it was the way he should have been raised.

It took some effort on Alex's part to break his abusive habits, but in the end he broke the chain of violence that had been following his family for generations. Under the Policy of Joint Agreement, not only was David spared a traumatic childhood like the one Alex had suffered, but Christine's love for Alex was restored.

Resolving Conflicts over Financial Planning

Instinctively, many of us seem to spend more than we earn. Perhaps we're all descendants of the same spendthrift ancestor, and we've inherited his undisciplined ways. But Shirley seemed to have inherited the trait in its purest form. Already in early childhood, she couldn't resist buying things she wanted. Her father tried to help her control her spending, but she would become so upset that he'd usually give in and hand her the money to buy what she wanted.

While Joe dated Shirley, he'd buy her gifts just to see her reaction. She seemed to live for her next gift from him. Joe's generosity brought out the best in her, and within six months they were head over heels in love with each other.

As an executive in a growing company, Joe earned very good wages, but they were not nearly enough to support Shirley's buying habits.

In the first few years of marriage, he justified many of her acquisitions as necessities for their new home. But Shirley wasn't satisfied with her initial purchases. She'd be off buying replacement items before some of the originals were even delivered. The closets in their home were soon so filled with her clothes that she had to give many away to make room for new purchases.

Joe became alarmed. "Shirley, I think it's time we discuss something. You're spending more than we can afford."

She was genuinely concerned. "Oh, Joe, are you having financial problems?"

"*We* are having financial problems! My income is better than ever, but I can't keep up with your spending," he complained. "We need to be on a budget. If I give you an allowance will you stick to it?"

"Sure," she responded. "That's okay with me." She agreed, but it was a reluctant agreement.

Joe worked out a budget for Shirley, but she didn't stick to it. When Joe brought up the subject, she shrugged it off as a bad month and promised to do better in the next month. But the next month was no better.

Joe decided to take matters into his own hands. "Shirley, I must put a stop to your irresponsible spending. I'm taking your name off our checking account and canceling your credit cards. I'm sorry, but it's the only way to solve the problem."

Shirley was terribly hurt. She knew she had a problem, but Joe was treating her like a child. Even though he gave her a generous cash allowance each week, she resented him for taking control of their finances without her agreement. It wasn't long before her cheerful outlook turned into bitterness and anger.

Joe experienced Shirley's state of conflict with both barrels. Within a month, they came to see me.

What should they do? How would you handle this problem?

Shirley had been spending money wildly, without Joe's enthusiastic agreement. That's what first got them into trouble. And they did negotiate an agreement, didn't they? Actually, Joe told Shirley what to do and she reluctantly agreed to do it. Then she didn't keep her end of the deal. She violated their agreement. In response, Joe canceled Shirley's credit cards, with not even a reluctant agreement on her part.

He had to protect their finances, didn't he? He was treating her like a child, but what else was he supposed to do: Sit by quietly while she dragged them both into bankruptcy?

This problem may hit close to home for you and your spouse. Your spouse may not be the spendthrift that Shirley was, but he or she spends enough to have you concerned. Before reading this book, you may have responded to this problem exactly the same way that Joe did—by trying to take control of the situation. But that's a pattern of behavior that will not solve your problem any more than it solved Joe and Shirley's problem. And it will cause you and your spouse to lose your love for each other.

The problem that Shirley and Joe faced is common. One spouse violates the Policy of Joint Agreement, so the other feels justified in violating it too. This tit-for-tat approach to marital conflict sends most marriages into the tank, but it seems fair at the time. After all, why should one spouse be mature when the other is being childish? Why shouldn't they both be childish?

> **Once they started to bargain with each other using the Policy of Joint Agreement, she felt in control of the process and the outcome.**

Let's rewind this story a bit to when Joe suggested that they follow a budget. Shirley agreed, but not enthusiastically. It was his budget. She felt that he imposed it on her. Her Giver had said yes, but her Taker harbored doubts, doubts that led her to disregard the budget. The first time this happened, it should have been clear that her Taker had not agreed to the bargain. They should have gone back to the bargaining table, this time with her Taker present.

In my counseling office, I asked Shirley how she felt about budgets. "I hate them!" she shot back.

"Then why did you agree to go on a budget?"

"To get Joe off my back. He had no right telling me what to do, and I knew at the time I wouldn't follow his little rules." She suddenly looked a bit guilty. "You won't tell Joe what I've just said, will you?"

Shirley's Taker had slipped out just long enough for me to get a glimpse of it, and it made everything crystal clear.

To make a long story short, I showed Joe how to bargain with Shirley instead of imposing his will on her. To reach an agreement that she would honor, he had to appeal to her self-centered side. He was not accustomed to this approach, nor was she used to expressing her self-centeredness openly. It took a while for them to learn how to compromise, but within a few months they had reached an agreement that Shirley followed.

Interestingly enough, it was very close to Joe's original plan. Shirley actually decided that the best way for her to control her spending was to get rid of her credit cards and access to their checking account. She shopped with the cash that she and Joe agreed they could afford.

You see, it wasn't that Joe's plan was so bad. That was not the issue. The problem occurred when Joe didn't negotiate with Shirley. It was his plan, not their plan. Once they started to bargain with each other using the Policy of Joint Agreement, she felt in control of the process and the outcome. And eventually she came to the same conclusion as Joe did. Now it was also her conclusion, and she agreed to it enthusiastically.

> **Crucial decisions should never be left to one spouse alone.**

To help Shirley learn new spending habits, I used a behavioral plan that monitored her spending over a period of three months. Prior to her agreement, she would never have followed through with that plan or any other plan, but this time she followed it perfectly and made changes that amazed everyone who knew her, particularly Joe.

Because financial planning is such an important marital issue, I spend quite a bit of time helping couples manage their money. I don't give financial or investment advice, because that's not where my training lies, but I do help couples agree on how they will spend their limited resources in ways that take the interests of both spouses into account. The Policy of Joint Agreement helps them reach that important goal.

Financial planning should take the interests of both spouses into account. Such crucial decisions should never be left to one spouse alone. Both spouses should learn to review their finances regularly and come to enthusiastic agreement as to how their income is spent.

This brings us to another common problem in marriage: how the money is earned. The Policy of Joint Agreement is a big help in showing couples how to spend the money they earn. But sometimes it's an even bigger help when they make career decisions.

Resolving Conflicts over Career-Related Choices

Like many other women, Renee admired ambitious men, and Jim was one of the most ambitious she had ever known. Though he had worked his way through college by taking two jobs, he had outstanding grades. And he was so well organized that, in spite of his busy schedule, he made a point of seeing her almost every day.

After their marriage, his career took off, and Renee was squeezed out of his schedule. When she complained to him about how little time they had together, he explained how important this phase of his career was and how he would have more time for her and his family in a few years.

Ten years and three children later, nothing had changed. Jim was an absentee husband and father. At a point of desperation, Renee made an appointment, without Jim, for advice. During the session, she confided that she'd fallen in love with another man and wouldn't be all that disappointed if her marriage to Jim ended in divorce.

How would you suggest solving Renee's problem?

Jim had not discussed his work schedule with Renee. And if he had, he would not have had her enthusiastic agreement.

Do you think a wife has a right to overrule her husband's work schedule? She does if the couple follows the Policy of Joint Agreement. In fact she has a right to overrule every move he makes. Without her agreement, he should not even leave for work in the morning.

The truth was, by the time Renee got to me, she didn't want Jim home any more than he was. The time when she wanted his companionship had passed, and unless he included her in his schedule soon, he might lose her entirely.

In spite of her reservations, however, Renee was willing to give her marriage one more chance. And she agreed to inform her husband about her new relationship and how it was threatening their marriage. Three days later Jim came to see me in a panic. "What can I do to save my marriage?" he asked.

Each decision made in marriage affects both husband and wife, so they need to consider each other's feelings when they make any decision, including decisions about their work schedules. But what should a couple do with an existing schedule that has not yet been agreed to? Should they continue with that schedule until they have an enthusiastic agreement for change? Or should they abandon it entirely and start from scratch?

Jim had gone down a path where so many decisions had been made without the Policy of Joint Agreement that backtracking seemed almost impossible. He worked long hours to be successful at what he did. How could he cut back and still get the job done? His responsibilities sometimes required travel that took him out of the country for a week or more. Missing those contacts might jeopardize everything he had worked so hard to accomplish, especially a promotion that was on the line.

> Each decision made in marriage affects both husband and wife, so they need to consider each other's feelings when they make any decision, including decisions about their work schedules.

But, fortunately, he agreed with me that unless he put Renee first, and followed the Policy of Joint Agreement with each decision he made, he would lose something much more important to him than his career.

So he put his career on the line. If changing jobs, or even changing careers was what it took to win Renee back, he was willing to do it. That willingness to follow the Policy of Joint Agreement, even if it meant losing his career, gave him the chance he needed to save his marriage.

Renee was surprised and impressed by Jim's reaction to the problem. She had always felt that his career was more important to him than she was. But now he was telling her that he would give up his career if that is what she wanted. That's not really what she wanted at all. She simply wanted to be his highest priority. She was willing to negotiate with him about the details of his career so that they could create a new lifestyle that enabled him to meet her emotional needs.

Renee was also impressed with the way Jim handled the revelation of her developing affair. She had been afraid to confront him about her growing feelings for another man, for fear he would divorce her on the spot and humiliate her in front of their children and her family. But he did the opposite. He never discussed with anyone else what she had told him, and her relationship with the "other man" had not yet progressed beyond her feelings. The man didn't even know she was interested.

From then on Jim and Renee made sure that at least fifteen hours a week were scheduled for undivided attention—the time they set aside to meet each other's most important emotional needs. And every Sunday afternoon they planned their activities and responsibilities of the week. Neither could make a unilateral decision about how to spend his or her time. And when Jim took a business trip away from home, Renee went with him. The Policy of Joint Agreement had helped them dodge a bullet.

How do you feel about each other's career? Are you in enthusiastic agreement about what your spouse is doing and the schedule that the job requires? If you follow the Policy of Joint Agreement, there may be some changes in your future, but I guarantee you that those changes will make you happier than you are now, more compatible, and in love with each other.

Key Principles

- When the interests of your friends and relatives and the interests of your spouse are in conflict, your spouse's interests should be given the highest priority. The Policy of Joint Agreement helps you maintain that perspective whenever you make decisions regarding your friends and relatives.

- Couples are wiser in the way they train their children when they agree on a training method.

- Both spouses should learn to review their finances regularly and come to enthusiastic agreement as to how their income is spent.

- Husbands and wives need to consider each other's feelings when they make any decision, including decisions about their work schedules.

Thinking It Through

1. In the last chapter, I encouraged you to practice following the Policy of Joint Agreement by deciding which items should be placed in your grocery cart. The idea was to practice making enthusiastic agreements using an issue that does not affect either of you emotionally. If you have completed that exercise, you should be ready to tackle some of the subjects I have introduced in this chapter. If you do, try to resolve at least one of them as a way to practice following the Policy of Joint Agreement. Be sure to follow the Four Guidelines for Successful Negotiation until you are able to find a solution.

2. The two most important categories of conflict in marriage are over emotional needs and over the Love Buster annoying behavior. An example of a conflict over an emotional need might be that one spouse would like more affection or sexual fulfillment or for love-making to be done in a certain way. An annoying behavior that might cause conflict could be one spouse staying at work too long or one spouse talking with friends on the telephone all evening. Most of the conflicts described in this chapter are examples of conflicts over annoying behavior.

   Use the Policy of Joint Agreement to try to resolve a conflict that you are having about one of your important emotional needs. Remember, the way the emotional need is to be met must meet the conditions of the Policy of Joint Agreement. That means that you must negotiate until you are able to discover a way to meet the need with enthusiasm. As I mentioned with the grocery cart example, one of the best negotiating strategies is to demonstrate that a particular solution is in the reluctant spouse's best interest, and to try it out to prove it (make sure it really is in your spouse's best interest or you may get only one chance!).

CONCLUSION

You have just been introduced to all the concepts I use whenever I try to save a marriage. If you apply them all to your marriage, you will do what most couples want to do but have failed to do— fall in love and stay in love. And that's what ultimately will save your marriage—the feeling of love. (For a quick review of these concepts, see appendix A.)

Romantic love, that feeling of incredible attraction, is the best litmus test of your success in giving each other the care and protection that you need. If you are both in love, your Takers are convinced that the relationship is a good deal for both of you, and they will not try to impose their destructive instincts on you. You will have free rein to provide each other the best of what you both have to offer.

When you are in love, your emotions help you meet each other's emotional needs. They provide instincts that you may not have even known you have—instincts to be affectionate, sexual, conversational, recreational, honest, and admiring. These all seem to come naturally when you are in love.

But when you fall out of love, your emotions work against your marriage. Everything that will help your marriage seems unnatural. That's why I've created these basic concepts—to help you do what it takes to restore your love for each other. Once your love is restored, these concepts will be much easier to apply and they will help you stay in love for the rest of your lives.

Habits for a Lifetime of Love

I have devoted my life to helping couples fall in love and stay in love. By following my advice hundreds of thousands, possibly millions, of couples have avoided the pain and disaster of divorce. And divorce *is* a disastrous outcome, especially when you consider how happy you can be together if you simply apply my basic concepts to your marriage.

What a pity it is that all couples do not know how to make Love Bank deposits and avoid withdrawals. They think that the love they feel for each other on their wedding day will carry them through life, regardless of what they do. Most of them don't realize that without habits of care and protection, they will lose that love, and along with it, their dream of a fulfilling marriage.

Now you have the basic tools to help you create what very few couples ever achieve—love that lasts a lifetime. And love is not all you will achieve. You will find that when you are in love with each other, your children will be happier and more successful, your career will flourish more than ever, your health will greatly improve, and your outlook on life will be optimistic and confident. There are so many advantages to being in love with each other that you simply must make it your highest priority. I encourage you and your spouse to become experts in the use of these basic concepts that will guarantee you a lifetime of love.

SUMMARY OF MY BASIC CONCEPTS TO HELP YOU FALL IN LOVE AND STAY IN LOVE

Basic Concept 1: The Love Bank

In my struggle to learn how to save marriages, I eventually discovered that the best way to do it was to teach couples how to fall in love—and stay in love—with each other. So I created the concept of the Love Bank to help couples understand how people fall in and out of love. This concept, perhaps more than any other that I have created, has helped couples realize that almost everything they do affects their love for each other either positively or negatively. That awareness has set most of them on a course of action that has preserved their love and saved their marriages.

Within each of us is a Love Bank that keeps track of the way people treat us. Everyone we know has an account and the things they do either deposit or withdraw love units from their accounts. It's the way your emotions encourage you to be with those who make you happy. When you associate someone with good feelings, deposits are made into that person's account in your Love Bank. And when the Love Bank reaches a certain level of deposits (the romantic-love threshold), the feeling of love is triggered. As long as your Love Bank balance remains above that threshold, you will experience the feeling of love. But when it falls below that threshold, you will lose that feeling. You will like anyone with a balance above zero, but you will only be in love with someone whose balance is above the love threshold.

Not only do your emotions encourage you to be with those who make you happy, they also discourage you from being with those who make you unhappy. Whenever you associate someone with bad feelings, withdrawals are made from your Love Bank. And if that person makes more withdrawals than deposits, his or her balance in your Love Bank can fall below zero. When that happens the Love Bank turns into the Hate Bank. You will dislike those with moderate negative balances, but if a balance falls below the hate threshold, you will hate the person.

Try living with a spouse you hate! Your emotions are doing everything they can to get you out of there—and divorce is one of the most logical ways to escape.

Couples usually ask for my advice when they are just about ready to give up on their marriage. Their Love Banks have been losing love units so long that they are now deeply in the red. And their negative Love Bank accounts make them feel uncomfortable just being in the same room with each other. They cannot imagine surviving marriage for another year, let alone ever being in love again.

But that's my job—to help them fall in love with each other again. I encourage them to stop making Love Bank withdrawals and start making Love Bank deposits. I created all of the remaining basic concepts to help couples achieve those objectives.

Basic Concept 2: Instincts and Habits

Instincts are behavioral patterns that we are born with, and habits are patterns that we learn. Both instincts and habits tend to be repeated again and again almost effortlessly. They are important in our discussion of what it takes to be in love because it's our behavior that makes deposits in and withdrawals from Love Banks, and our instincts and habits make up most of our behavior.

Instincts and habits can make Love Bank deposits, so it is imperative to learn those habits because once they are learned, deposits in your spouse's Love Bank are made repeatedly and almost effortlessly.

Unfortunately, many of our instincts and habits, such as angry outbursts, contribute to Love Bank withdrawals. Since they are repeated so often, they play a very important role in the annihilation of Love Bank accounts. If we are to stop Love Bank withdrawals, we must somehow stop destructive instincts and habits in their tracks. Instincts are harder to stop than habits, but they can both be avoided.

As we discuss the remaining concepts, keep in mind the value of a good habit and the harm of a bad habit, because their effect on Love Bank balances is multiplied by repetition.

Basic Concept 3: The Most Important Emotional Needs

What's the fastest way to deposit love units into each other's Love Bank? I interviewed literally hundreds of couples trying to find the answer to this question when I was first learning how to save marriages. Eventually the answer became clear to me—you must meet each other's most important emotional needs.

You and your spouse fell in love with each other because you made each other very happy, and you made each other happy because you met some of each other's important emotional needs. The only way you and your spouse will stay in love is to keep meeting those needs. Even when the feeling of love begins to fade, or when it's gone entirely, it's not necessarily gone for good. It can be recovered whenever you both go back to making large Love Bank deposits.

First, be sure you know what each other's most important emotional needs are by completing the Emotional Needs Questionnaire (appendix B). Then learn to meet the needs that are rated the highest in a way that is fulfilling to your spouse, and enjoyable for you too.

It's likely that you and your spouse do not prioritize your needs in the same order of importance. A highly important need for you may not be as important to your spouse. So you may find yourself trying to meet needs that seem unimportant to you. But your spouse depends on you to meet those needs, and it's the most effective and efficient way for you to make large deposits in your spouse's Love Bank.

Basic Concept 4: The Policy of Undivided Attention

Unless you and your spouse schedule time each week for undivided attention, it will be impossible to meet each other's most important emotional needs. To help you and your spouse clear space in your schedule for each other, I have written the **Policy of Undivided Attention: Give your spouse your undivided attention a minimum of fifteen hours each week, using the time to meet the emotional needs of affection, sexual fulfillment, conversation, and recreational companionship.** This policy will help you avoid one of the most common mistakes in marriage—neglecting each other.

This basic concept not only helps guarantee that you will meet each other's emotional needs but also unlocks the door to the use of all the other basic concepts. Without time for undivided attention, you will not be able to avoid Love Busters and you will not be able to negotiate effectively. Time for undivided attention is the necessary ingredient for everything that's important in marriage.

And yet, as soon as most couples marry, and especially when children arrive, couples usually replace their time together with activities of lesser importance. You probably did the same thing. You tried to meet each other's needs with "leftover" time, but sadly, there wasn't much time left over. Your lack of private time together may have become a great cause of unhappiness, and yet you felt incapable of preventing it. You may have also found yourself bottling up your honest expression of feelings because there was just no appropriate time to talk.

Make your time to be alone with each other your highest priority—that way it will never be replaced by activities of lesser value. Your career, your time with your children, maintenance of your home, and a host of other demands will all compete for your time together. But if you follow the Policy of Undivided Attention, you will not let anything steal from you those precious and crucial hours together.

It is essential to (a) spend time away from children and friends whenever you give each other your undivided attention; (b) use the time to meet each other's emotional needs of affection, conversation, recreational companionship, and sexual fulfillment; and (c) schedule at least fifteen hours together each week. When you were dating, you gave each other this kind of attention and you fell in love. When people have affairs, they also give each other this kind of attention to keep their love for each other alive. Why should courtship and affairs be the only times love is created? Why can't it happen throughout marriage as well? It can, if you set aside time every week to give each other undivided attention.

Basic Concept 5: Love Busters

When you meet each other's most important emotional needs, you become each other's source of greatest happiness. But if you are not careful, you can also become each other's source of greatest unhappiness.

It's pointless to deposit love units if you withdraw them right away. So, in addition to meeting important emotional needs, you must also be sure to protect your spouse. Guard your account in your spouse's Love Bank from withdrawals by paying attention to how your everyday behavior can make each other unhappy.

You and your spouse were born to be demanding, disrespectful, angry, annoying, and dishonest. These are normal human traits that I call Love Busters because they destroy the feeling of love spouses have for each other. But if you promise to avoid being the cause of your spouse's unhappiness, you will do whatever it takes to overcome these destructive tendencies for your spouse's protection. By eliminating Love Busters, you will not only be protecting your spouse, but you will also be preserving your spouse's love for you.

Basic Concept 6: The Policy of Radical Honesty

If you and your spouse are to be in love with each other, you must give honesty special attention. That's because it plays such an important role in the creation of love. It is one of the ten most important emotional needs, so when it's met, it can trigger the feeling of love. On the other hand, its counterpart, dishonesty, is a Love Buster—it destroys love.

But there is another reason that honesty is crucial in creating love. Honesty is the only way that you and your spouse will ever come to understand each other. Without honesty, the adjustments that are crucial to making each other happy and avoiding unhappiness cannot be made.

It isn't easy to be honest. Honesty is an unpopular value these days, and most couples have not made this commitment to each other. Many marriage counselors and clergymen argue that honesty is not always the best policy. They believe that it's cruel to disclose past indiscretions and it's selfish to make such disclosures. While it makes you feel better to get a mistake off your chest, it causes your partner to suffer. So, they argue, the truly caring thing to do is to lie about your mistakes or at least keep them tucked away.

And if it's compassionate to lie about sins of the past, why isn't it also compassionate to lie about sins of the present—or future? To my way of thinking, it's like letting the proverbial camel's nose under the tent. Eventually you will be dining with the camel. Either honesty is always right, or you'll always have an excuse for being dishonest.

To help remind couples how important honesty is in marriage, I have written the **Policy of Radical Honesty: Reveal to your spouse as much information about yourself as you know— your thoughts, feelings, habits, likes, dislikes, personal history, daily activities, and plans for the future.**

Self-imposed honesty with your spouse is essential to your marriage's safety and success. Not only will honesty bring you closer to each other emotionally, it will also prevent the creation of destructive habits that are kept secret from your spouse.

Basic Concept 7: The Giver and Taker

Have you ever thought that your spouse is possessed? One moment he or she is loving and thoughtful, and the next you are faced with selfishness and thoughtlessness. Trust me, it's not a demon you're up against, it's the two sides of our personalities. I call them the Giver and the Taker.

All of us want to make a difference in the lives of others. We want others to be happy and we want to contribute to their happiness. When we feel that way, our Giver is influencing us. The Giver's rule is **do whatever you can to make others happy and avoid anything that makes others unhappy, even if it makes you unhappy.** It encourages us to use that rule in our relationships with other people.

But we also want the best for ourselves. We want to be happy, too. When we feel that way, our Taker is influencing us. The Taker's rule is **do whatever you can to make you happy, and avoid anything that makes you unhappy, even if it makes others unhappy.** If that rule makes sense to you, it's because your Taker is in control.

These two primitive aspects of our personality are usually balanced in our dealings with others, but in marriage they tend to take turns being in charge. And that leads to most of the problems that couples encounter. If we take the advice of our Giver, we are willing to suffer to make our spouse happy, and if we take the advice of our Taker, we are willing to let our spouse suffer to make us happy. In either case the advice we are given is shortsighted because someone always gets hurt.

Basic Concept 8: The Three States of Mind in Marriage

The Giver and Taker create moods that I call states of mind. These states of mind have a tremendous influence on the way a husband and wife try to resolve conflicts. Each of the three states of mind discourages negotiation. That's what makes negotiation, in general, so tough in marriage.

When we are happy and in love, we are usually in the **state of intimacy.** That state of mind is controlled by the Giver, which encourages us to follow the Giver's rule: *Do whatever you can to make your spouse happy and avoid anything that makes your spouse unhappy, even if it makes you unhappy.* That rule can lead to habits that may be good for your spouse but can be disastrous for you because you are not negotiating with your own interests in mind.

Sadly, flawed agreements made in the state of intimacy can lead to our own unhappiness, and that in turn wakes the slumbering Taker. As long as we are happy, our Taker has nothing to do, but when we start feeling unhappy, our Taker rises to our rescue and triggers the **state of conflict.** With the Taker now in charge, we are encouraged to follow the rule: *Do whatever you can to make you happy, and avoid anything that makes you unhappy, even if it makes others unhappy.* The Taker also encourages you to be demanding, disrespectful, and angry in an effort to force your spouse to make you happy. Fighting is the Taker's favorite "negotiating" strategy.

When fighting doesn't work, and we are still unhappy, the Taker encourages us to take a new course of action that triggers the **state of withdrawal.** Instead of trying to force our spouse to make us happy, our Taker wants us to give up on our spouse entirely. We don't want our spouse to do anything for us and we certainly don't want to do anything for our spouse. In this state of mind we are emotionally divorced.

How can couples work their way back to the state of intimacy once they find themselves trapped in the state of withdrawal? And once they are back, how can they stay there? The answers to those questions are found in basic concept 9.

Basic Concept 9: The Policy of Joint Agreement

Marital instincts do not lead to fair negotiation. They lead to either giving away the store (state of intimacy) or robbing the bank (state of conflict). And in the state of withdrawal, no one even feels like negotiating. Yet in order to meet each other's most important needs and avoid Love Busters consistently and effectively, fair negotiation is crucial in marriage.

You need a rule to help you override the shortsighted advice of your Giver and Taker. Their advice is shortsighted because regardless of the rule, someone gets hurt. We get hurt when we follow the Giver's advice, and our spouse gets hurt when we follow the Taker's advice. So I've created a rule to guarantee that no one gets hurt, and that's the ultimate goal in fair negotiation. I call this rule the Policy of Joint Agreement: **Never do anything without the enthusiastic agreement of your spouse.**

Almost everything you and your spouse do affects each other. So it's very important to know what that effect will be before you actually do it. The Policy of Joint Agreement will help you remember to consult with each other to be sure you avoid being the cause of each other's unhappiness. It also makes negotiation necessary, regardless of your state of mind. If you agree to this policy, you will not be able to do anything without the enthusiastic agreement of the other, so it forces you to discuss your plans and negotiate with each other's feelings in mind. Without safe and pleasant negotiation, you will simply not be able to reach an enthusiastic agreement.

The Policy of Joint Agreement, combined with the Policy of Radical Honesty, helps you create an open and integrated lifestyle, one that will guarantee your love for each other. These policies also prevent the creation of a secret second life where infidelity, the greatest threat to your marriage, can grow like mold in a damp, dark cellar.

Basic Concept 10: Four Guidelines for Successful Negotiation

If you and your spouse are in conflict about anything, I recommend that you do nothing until you can both agree enthusiastically about a resolution. But how should you go about reaching that resolution? I suggest you follow four essential guidelines:

Guideline 1: Set ground rules to make negotiation pleasant and safe.

Ground rule 1: Try to be pleasant and cheerful throughout negotiations.

Ground rule 2: Put safety first. Do not make demands, show disrespect, or become angry when you negotiate, even if your spouse makes demands, shows disrespect, or becomes angry with you.

Ground rule 3: If you reach an impasse and you do not seem to be getting anywhere, or if one of you is starting to make demands, show disrespect, or become angry, stop negotiating and come back to the issue later.

Guideline 2: Identify the problem from both perspectives with mutual respect for those perspectives.

Guideline 3: Brainstorm with abandon—give your creativity a chance to discover solutions that would make you both happy. Carry a pad and pencil with you to jot down ideas as you think of them throughout the day.

Guideline 4: Choose the solution that best meets the conditions of the Policy of Joint Agreement—mutual and enthusiastic agreement. Whenever a conflict arises, keep in mind the importance of finding a solution that deposits as many love units as possible, while avoiding withdrawals. And be sure that the way you find that solution also deposits love units and avoids withdrawals.

EMOTIONAL NEEDS
QUESTIONNAIRE

This questionnaire is designed to help you determine your most important emotional needs and evaluate your spouse's effectiveness in meeting those needs. Answer all the questions as candidly as possible. Do not try to minimize any needs that you feel have been unmet. If your answers require more space, use and attach a separate sheet of paper.

Your spouse should complete a separate Emotional Needs Questionnaire so that you can discover his or her needs and evaluate your effectiveness in meeting those needs.

When you have completed this questionnaire, go through it a second time to be certain your answers accurately reflect your feelings. Do not erase your original answers, but cross them out lightly so that your spouse can see the corrections and discuss them with you.

The final page of this questionnaire asks you to identify and rank five of the ten needs in order of their importance to you. The most important emotional needs are those that give you the most pleasure when met and frustrate you the most when unmet. Resist the temptation to identify as most important only those needs that your spouse is *not* presently meeting. Include *all* your emotional needs in your consideration of those that are most important.

You have the permission of the publisher to photocopy the questionnaire for use in your own marriage. I recommend that you enlarge it 125 percent so that you'll have plenty of room to write in your responses.

1. **Affection.** Showing love through words, cards, gifts, hugs, kisses, and courtesies; creating an environment that clearly and repeatedly expresses love.

   A. **Need for affection:** Indicate how much you need affection by circling the appropriate number.

   | 0 | 1 | 2 | 3 | 4 | 5 | 6 |

   I have no need
   for affection

   I have a moderate
   need for affection

   I have a great need
   for affection

   If or when your spouse is *not* affectionate with you, how do you feel? (Circle the appropriate letter.)
   a. Very unhappy
   b. Somewhat unhappy
   c. Neither happy nor unhappy
   d. Happy not to be shown affection

   If or when your spouse is affectionate to you, how do you feel? (Circle the appropriate letter.)
   a. Very happy
   b. Somewhat happy
   c. Neither happy nor unhappy
   d. Unhappy to be shown affection

   B. **Evaluation of spouse's affection:** Indicate your satisfaction with your spouse's affection toward you by circling the appropriate number.

   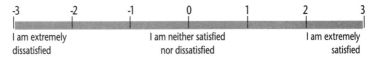

   | -3 | -2 | -1 | 0 | 1 | 2 | 3 |

   I am extremely
   dissatisfied

   I am neither satisfied
   nor dissatisfied

   I am extremely
   satisfied

   My spouse gives me all the affection I need.   Yes   No

   If your answer is no, how often would you like your spouse to be affectionate with you?

   _____ (write number) times each day/week/month (circle one).

   I like the way my spouse gives me affection.   Yes   No

   If your answer is no, explain how your need for affection could be better satisfied in your marriage. _____
   _____
   _____
   _____
   _____

2. **Sexual Fulfillment.** A sexual relationship that brings out a predictably enjoyable sexual response in both of you that is frequent enough for both of you.

   A. **Need for sexual fulfillment:** Indicate how much you need sexual fulfillment by circling the appropriate number.

   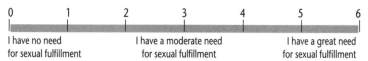

0	1	2	3	4	5	6

   I have no need   I have a moderate need   I have a great need
   for sexual fulfillment   for sexual fulfillment   for sexual fulfillment

   If or when your spouse *is not* willing to engage in sexual relations with you, how do you feel? (Circle the appropriate letter.)
   a. Very unhappy   c. Neither happy nor unhappy
   b. Somewhat unhappy   d. Happy not to engage in
                                 sexual relations

   If or when your spouse engages in sexual relations with you, how do you feel? (Circle the appropriate letter.)
   a. Very happy   c. Neither happy nor unhappy
   b. Somewhat happy   d. Unhappy to engage in
                                 sexual relations

   B. **Evaluation of sexual relations with your spouse:** Indicate your satisfaction with your spouse's sexual relations with you by circling the appropriate number.

-3	-2	-1	0	1	2	3

   I am extremely   I am neither satisfied   I am extremely
   dissatisfied   nor dissatisfied   satisfied

   My spouse has sexual relations with me as often as I need. Yes   No

   If your answer is no, how often would you like your spouse to have sex with you?

   _____ (write number) times each day/week/month (circle one).

   I like the way my spouse has sexual relations with me. Yes   No

   If your answer is no, explain how your need for sexual fulfillment could be better satisfied in your marriage._____
   _____
   _____
   _____

3. Conversation. Talking about events of the day, feelings, and plans; avoiding angry or judgmental statements or dwelling on past mistakes; showing interest in your favorite topics of conversation; balancing conversation; using it to inform, investigate, and understand you; and giving you undivided attention.

A. **Need for conversation:** Indicate how much you need conversation by circling the appropriate number.

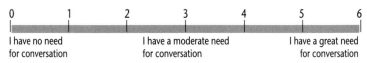

| 0 | 1 | 2 | 3 | 4 | 5 | 6 |

I have no need
for conversation

I have a moderate need
for conversation

I have a great need
for conversation

If or when your spouse *is not* willing to talk with you, how do you feel? (Circle the appropriate letter.)
a. Very unhappy   c. Neither happy nor unhappy
b. Somewhat unhappy   d. Happy not to talk

If or when your spouse talks to you, how do you feel? (Circle the appropriate letter.)
a. Very happy   c. Neither happy nor unhappy
b. Somewhat happy   d. Unhappy to talk

B. **Evaluation of conversation with your spouse:** Indicate your satisfaction with your spouse's conversation with you by circling the appropriate number.

| -3 | -2 | -1 | 0 | 1 | 2 | 3 |

I am extremely
dissatisfied

I am neither satisfied
nor dissatisfied

I am extremely
satisfied

My spouse talks to me as often as I need. Yes   No

If your answer is no, how often would you like your spouse to talk to you?

_____ (write number) times each day/week/month (circle one).

_____ (write number) hours each day/week/month (circle one).

I like the way my spouse talks to me. Yes   No

If your answer is no, explain how your need for conversation could be better satisfied in your marriage. _____

_____

_____

4. Recreational Companionship. Developing interest in your favorite recreational activities, learning to be proficient in them, and joining you in those activities. If any prove to be unpleasant to your spouse after an effort has been made, negotiating new recreational activities that are mutually enjoyable.

A. **Need for recreational companionship:** Indicate how much you need recreational companionship by circling the appropriate number.

| 0 | 1 | 2 | 3 | 4 | 5 | 6 |

I have no need for recreational companionship   I have a moderate need for recreational companionship   I have a great need for recreational companionship

If or when your spouse *is not* willing to join you in recreational activities, how do you feel? (Circle the appropriate letter.)

a. Very unhappy   c. Neither happy nor unhappy
b. Somewhat unhappy   d. Happy not to include my spouse

If or when your spouse joins you in recreational activities, how do you feel? (Circle the appropriate letter.)

a. Very unhappy   c. Neither happy nor unhappy
b. Somewhat unhappy   d. Unhappy to include my spouse

B. **Evaluation of recreational companionship with your spouse:** Indicate your satisfaction with your spouse's recreational companionship by circling the appropriate number.

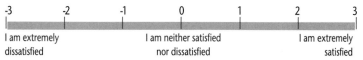

| -3 | -2 | -1 | 0 | 1 | 2 | 3 |

I am extremely dissatisfied   I am neither satisfied nor dissatisfied   I am extremely satisfied

My spouse joins me in recreational activities as often as I need.   Y   N

If your answer is no, how often would you like your spouse to join you in recreational activities?

_____ (write number) times each day/week/month (circle one).

_____ (write number) hours each day/week/month (circle one).

I like the way my spouse joins me in recreational activities.   Yes   No

If your answer is no, explain how your need for recreational companionship could be better satisfied in your marriage._____
_____
_____

5. **Honesty and Openness.** Revealing positive and negative feelings, events of the past, daily events and schedule, plans for the future; not leaving you with a false impression; answering your questions truthfully.

A. **Need for honesty and openness:** Indicate how much you need honesty and openness by circling the appropriate number.

| 0 | 1 | 2 | 3 | 4 | 5 | 6 |

I have no need   I have a moderate need   I have a great need
for honesty and openness   for honesty and openness   for honesty and openness

If or when your spouse *is not* open and honest with you, how do you feel? (Circle the appropriate letter.)
a. Very unhappy
b. Somewhat unhappy
c. Neither happy nor unhappy
d. Happy that my spouse isn't honest and open

If or when your spouse is open and honest with you, how do you feel? (Circle the appropriate letter.)
a. Very happy
b. Somewhat happy
c. Neither happy nor unhappy
d. Unhappy that my spouse is honest and open

B. **Evaluation of spouse's honesty and openness:** Indicate your satisfaction with your spouse's honesty and openness by circling the appropriate number.

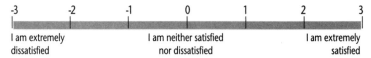

| -3 | -2 | -1 | 0 | 1 | 2 | 3 |

I am extremely   I am neither satisfied   I am extremely
dissatisfied   nor dissatisfied   satisfied

In which of the following areas of honesty and openness would you like to see improvement from your spouse? (Circle the letters that apply to you.)
a. Sharing positive and negative emotional reactions to significant aspects of life
b. Sharing information regarding his/her personal history
c. Sharing information about his/her daily activities
d. Sharing information about his/her future schedule and plans

If you circled any of the above, explain how your need for honesty and openness could be better satisfied in your marriage._____
_____
_____

6. **Attractiveness of Spouse.** Keeping physically fit with diet and excercise; wearing hair, clothing, and (if female) makeup in a way that you find attractive and tasteful.

A. **Need for an attractive spouse:** Indicate how much you need an attractive spouse by circling the appropriate number.

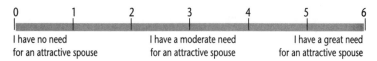

| 0 | 1 | 2 | 3 | 4 | 5 | 6 |

I have no need   I have a moderate need   I have a great need
for an attractive spouse   for an attractive spouse   for an attractive spouse

If or when your spouse *is not* willing to make the most of his or her physical attractiveness, how do you feel? (Circle the appropriate letter.)
a. Very unhappy
b. Somewhat unhappy
c. Neither happy nor unhappy
d. Happy he or she does not make an effort

When your spouse makes the most of his or her physical attractiveness, how do you feel? (Circle the appropriate letter.)
a. Very happy
b. Somewhat happy
c. Neither happy nor unhappy
d. Unhappy to see that he or she makes an effort

B. **Evaluation of spouse's attractiveness:** Indicate your satisfaction with your spouse's attractiveness by circling the appropriate number.

| -3 | -2 | -1 | 0 | 1 | 2 | 3 |

I am extremely   I am neither satisfied   I am extremely
dissatisfied   nor dissatisfied   satisfied

In which of the following characteristics of attractiveness would you like to see improvement from your spouse? (Circle the letters that apply.)
a. Physical fitness and normal weight
b. Attractive choice of clothes
c. Attractive hairstyle
d. Good physical hygiene
e. Attractive facial makeup
f. Other _____

If you circled any of the above, explain how your need for an attractive spouse could be better satisfied in your marriage._____
_____
_____
_____

7. **Financial Support.** Provision of the financial resources to house, feed, and clothe your family at a standard of living acceptable to you, but avoiding travel and working hours that are unacceptable to you.

   A. **Need for financial support:** Indicate how much you need financial support by circling the appropriate number.

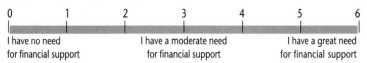

| 0 | 1 | 2 | 3 | 4 | 5 | 6 |

I have no need   I have a moderate need   I have a great need
for financial support   for financial support   for financial support

     If or when your spouse *is not* willing to support you financially, how do you feel? (Circle the appropriate letter.)

     a. Very unhappy   c. Neither happy nor unhappy
     b. Somewhat unhappy   d. Happy not to be financially
                                supported

     If or when your spouse supports you financially, how do you feel? (Circle the appropriate letter.)

     a. Very happy   c. Neither happy nor unhappy
     b. Somewhat happy   d. Unhappy to be financially
                                supported

   B. **Evaluation of spouse's financial support:** Indicate your satisfaction with your spouse's financial support by circling the appropriate number.

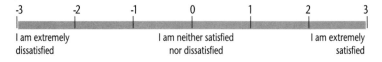

| -3 | -2 | -1 | 0 | 1 | 2 | 3 |

I am extremely   I am neither satisfied   I am extremely
dissatisfied   nor dissatisfied   satisfied

     How much money would you like your spouse to earn to support you?

     _____

     How many hours each week would you like your spouse to work? _____

     If your spouse is not earning as much as you would like, is not working the hours you would like, does not budget the way you would like, or does not earn an income the way you would like, explain how your need for financial support could be better satisfied in your marriage._____

     _____
     _____
     _____
     _____

8. **Domestic support.** Creation of a home environment for you that offers a refuge from the stresses of life; managing the home and care of the children—if any are at home—including but not limited to cooking meals, washing dishes, washing and ironing clothes, and housecleaning.

A. **Need for domestic support:** Indicate how much you need domestic support by circling the appropriate number.

| 0 | 1 | 2 | 3 | 4 | 5 | 6 |

I have no need for domestic support   I have a moderate need for domestic support   I have a great need for domestic support

If your spouse *is not* willing to provide you with domestic support, how do you feel? (Circle the appropriate letter.)
a. Very unhappy
b. Somewhat unhappy
c. Neither happy nor unhappy
d. Happy not to have domestic support

If or when your spouse provides you with domestic support, how do you feel? (Circle the appropriate letter.)
a. Very happy
b. Somewhat happy
c. Neither happy nor unhappy
d. Unhappy to have domestic support

B. **Evaluation of spouse's domestic support:** Indicate your satisfaction with your spouse's domestic support by circling the appropriate number.

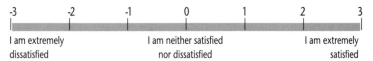

| -3 | -2 | -1 | 0 | 1 | 2 | 3 |

I am extremely dissatisfied   I am neither satisfied nor dissatisfied   I am extremely satisfied

My spouse provides me with all the domestic support I need. Yes   No

I like the way my spouse provides domestic support. Yes   No

If your answer is no to either of the above questions, explain how your need for domestic support could be better satisfied in your marriage._____

_____

_____

_____

_____

9. Family commitment. Scheduling sufficient time and energy for the moral and educational development of your children; reading to them, taking them on frequent outings, educating himself or herself in appropriate child-training methods and discussing those methods with you; avoiding any child-training method or disciplinary action that does not have your enthusiastic support.

    A. Need for family commitment: Indicate how much you need family commitment by circling the appropriate number.

0	1	2	3	4	5	6

I have no need
for family commitment

I have a moderate need
for family commitment

I have a great need
for family commitment

If or when your spouse *is not* willing to provide family commitment, how do you feel? (Circle the appropriate letter.)

a. Very unhappy   c. Neither happy nor unhappy

b. Somewhat unhappy   d. Happy he or she is not involved

If or when your spouse provides family commitment, how do you feel? (Circle the appropriate letter.)

a. Very happy   c. Neither happy nor unhappy

b. Somewhat happy   d. Unhappy he or she is involved in the family

    B. Evaluation of spouse's family commitment: Indicate your satisfaction with your spouse's family commitment by circling the appropriate number.

-3	-2	-1	0	1	2	3

I am extremely
dissatisfied

I am neither satisfied
nor dissatisfied

I am extremely
satisfied

My spouse commits enough time to the family.   Yes   No

If your answer is no, how often would you like your spouse to join in family activities?

_____ (write number) times each day/week/month (circle one).

_____ (write number) hours each day/week/month (circle one).

I like the way my spouse spends time with the family.   Yes   No

If your answer is no, explain how your need for family commitment could be better satisfied in your marriage._____

10. Admiration. Respecting, valuing, and appreciating you; rarely critical; and expressing admiration to you clearly and often.

A. Need for admiration: Indicate how much you need admiration by circling the appropriate number.

0	1	2	3	4	5	6

I have no need   I have a moderate need   I have a great need
for admiration   for admiration   for admiration

If or when your spouse *does not* admire you, how do you feel? (Circle the appropriate letter.)
a. Very unhappy
b. Somewhat unhappy
c. Neither happy nor unhappy
d. Happy not to be admired

If or when your spouse does admire you, how do you feel? (Circle the appropriate letter.)
a. Very happy
b. Somewhat happy
c. Neither happy nor unhappy
d. Unhappy to be admired

B. Evaluation of spouse's admiration: Indicate your satisfaction with your spouse's admiration of you by circling the appropriate number.

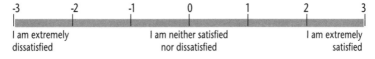

-3	-2	-1	0	1	2	3

I am extremely   I am neither satisfied   I am extremely
dissatisfied   nor dissatisfied   satisfied

My spouse gives me all the admiration I need.   Yes   No

If your answer is no, how often would you like your spouse to admire you?
_____ (write number) times each day/week/month (circle one).

I like the way my spouse admires me.   Yes   No

If your answer is no, explain how your need for admiration could be better satisfied in your marriage._____

_____

_____

_____

_____

_____

Ranking of Your Emotional Needs

The ten basic emotional needs are listed below. There is also space for you to add other emotional needs that you feel are essential to your marital happiness.

In the space provided before each need, write a number from 1 to 5 that ranks the need's importance to your happiness. Write a 1 before the most important need, a 2 before the next most important, and so on until you have ranked your five most important needs.

To help you rank these needs, imagine that you will have only one need met in your marriage. Which would make you the happiest, knowing that all the others would go unmet? That need should be 1. If only two needs will be met, what would your second selection be? Which five needs, when met, would make you the happiest?

____ Affection

____ Sexual Fulfillment

____ Conversation

____ Recreational Companionship

____ Honesty and Openness

____ Attractiveness of Spouse

____ Financial Support

____ Domestic Support

____ Family Commitment

____ Admiration

____ _____

____ _____

Agreement to Meet
the Most Important Emotional Needs

This Agreement is made this_____ day of_____ ,

between_____and_____ ,

 whereby it is mutually agreed:

_____ will learn to meet the following

emotional needs of_____ :

     1._____

     2._____

     3._____

     4._____

     5._____

_____ will learn to meet the following

emotional needs of_____ :

     1._____

     2._____

     3._____

     4._____

     5._____

 In Witness Whereof, the parties hereto have signed this agreement on the day

and year first above written:

_____   _____

     His signature   Her signature

Time for Undivided Attention Worksheet

For the Week of _____

Please report the time you give undivided attention to each other. You must be without friends, relatives, or children and must use the time to engage in conversation, affection, sex, or recreational activities that promote undivided attention.

First, schedule time to be together by completing the Planned Time Together part of this report. The total for the week should add up to fifteen hours or more. Then, as the week unfolds, complete the Actual Time Together part of the report. The estimate of time actually given to undivided attention depends on how each of you feels about the attention given. While you may have been together for two hours, one of you may feel only half of the time was given to undivided attention, while the other may feel that the entire two hours qualified. Because of this common difference of opinion, each of you is to provide your own estimate. In the last column, the lower estimate is to be entered. If the planned activity was canceled, explain why under Actual Activities.

At the end of the week, the total of the Lower Estimate column should be entered on the Time for Undivided Attention Graph. It should be fifteen hours or more if you want to sustain romantic love in your marriage.

Planned Time Together

Planned Date	Planned Time (from–to)	Total Planned Time
____	____	____
____	____	____
____	____	____
____	____	____
____	____	____
____	____	____
____	____	____
____	____	____
Total Time for the Week	____	

Actual Time Together

Planned Activities	Actual Activities	Her Estimate	His Estimate	Lower Estimate
____	____	____	____	____
____	____	____	____	____
____	____	____	____	____
____	____	____	____	____
____	____	____	____	____
____	____	____	____	____
____	____	____	____	____
____	____	____	____	____
			Total Time for the Week	____

Time for Undivided Attention Graph

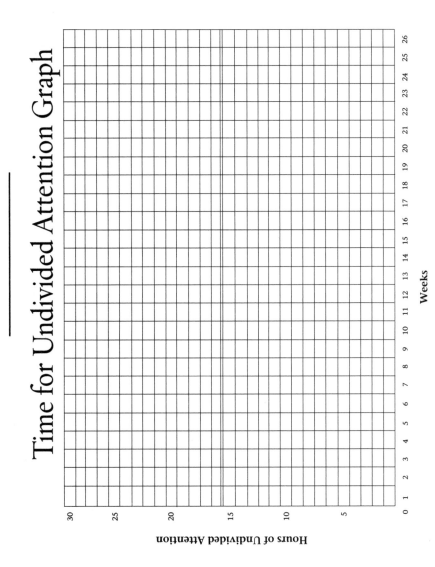

Hours of Undivided Attention

Weeks

PERSONAL HISTORY
QUESTIONNAIRE

Please answer all of the following questions as honestly and thoughtfully as possible. If your answer requires additional space, use another sheet of paper.

When answering these questions, it is important to remember the Rule of Honesty and its five parts:

The Rule of Honesty for Successful Marriage

Reveal to your spouse as much information about yourself as you know—your thoughts, feelings, habits, likes, dislikes, personal history, daily activities, and plans for the future

1. *Emotional honesty:* Reveal your emotional reactions—both positive and negative—to the events of your life, particularly to your spouse's behavior.
2. *Historical honesty:* Reveal information about your personal history, particularly events that demonstrate personal weakness and failure.
3. *Current honesty:* Reveal information about the events of your day. Provide your spouse with a calendar of your activities, with special emphasis on those that may affect your spouse.
4. *Future honesty:* Reveal your thoughts and plans regarding future activities and objectives.
5. *Complete honesty:* Do not leave your spouse with a false impression about your thoughts, feelings, habits, likes, dislikes, personal history, daily activities, or plans for the future. Do not deliberately keep personal information from your spouse.

I agree to consider this information confidential and will not share any information revealed in this questionnaire to anyone without my spouse's permission. I also agree to reward honesty and not punish my spouse for revealing any new information to me that I may find upsetting.

Signature: _____ Date_____

Health History

List childhood diseases, injuries, or operations:

_____

_____

List past adult diseases, injuries, or operations:

_____

_____

List present medical problems (include high blood pressure, arthritis, migraine headaches, etc.):

_____

_____

When did you have your last complete physical examination?

_____

What were the results? Did the doctor find a medical problem or are you generally in good health?

_____

_____

How long does it usually take you to fall asleep when you go to bed at night? _____ How many hours do you usually sleep?_____

How often do you awaken during the night?_____
How long does it take to get back to sleep? _____

How many pounds have you gained and/or lost in the past year?

_____

_____

Describe any of your past and present diet programs:

_____

_____

_____

Describe your current exercise program:

_____

_____

What drugs do you presently take, what dosages, how often, and for what conditions?

_____

_____

_____

Have you ever been hospitalized or received therapy for a mental disorder? If so, list hospital(s) and/or therapist(s) and approximate dates:

_____

_____

Do you now have or have you ever had venereal disease? If so, when and what were the conditions?

_____

_____

_____

For the wife: When did you have your first period? _____ Are your periods regular? _____ Are they comfortable? _____ Do they cause you to feel depressed, anxious, or irritable? _____

Family History

Mother's name: _____

age:_____ occupation:_____ education: _____

How did she punish you?

_____

_____

How did she reward you?

_____

_____

What behaviors did she punish?

_____

_____

What behaviors did she reward?

_____

_____

How would others describe your mother?

_____

_____

How would you describe your mother?

_____

_____

What activities did you do with your mother when you were a child?

_____

_____

How did you get along with your mother?

_____

_____

_____

Father's name: _____

age:_____ occupation:_____ education: _____

How did he punish you?

_____

_____

How did he reward you?

_____

_____

What behaviors did he punish?

_____

_____

What behaviors did he reward?

_____

_____

How would others describe your father?

_____

_____

How would you describe your father?

_____

_____

What activities did you do with your father when you were a child?

_____

_____

How did you get along with your father?

_____

_____

For each of your brother(s) and sister(s), give name, birth date, and how you got along with him/her when you were growing up together:

_____

_____

_____

Does (did) your mother or father favor one child? If so, who and why do you think they favored that child?

_____

_____

Were your mother and father divorced? If so, how old were you and what do you know about the reasons they divorced?

_____

_____

How do (did) your mother and father get along?

_____

_____

Was your father or mother (or both) alcoholic? If so, how did it affect your childhood?

_____

_____

Describe any instances of physical violence or sexual advances inflicted on you by a parent or siblings when you were a child.

_____

_____

_____

If you were raised by a stepparent or foster parents, please describe your most important experiences with them.

_____

_____

_____

Educational History

What preschool(s) did you attend?

_____

Describe any significant experiences there:

_____

_____

What elementary school(s) did you attend?

_____

Were you a good student?_____ Describe any significant experiences at your elementary school:

_____

_____

What middle and/or secondary school(s) did you attend?

_____

What were your grades?_____ Describe any significant experiences at your middle school or secondary school:

_____

_____

What college(s) or vocational school(s) did you attend?

_____

What were your grades?_____ Describe any significant experiences at college or vocational school:

_____

_____

What was your major or specialization?_____

Give degree and date earned: _____

What postgraduate school(s) did you attend?

_____

What were your grades?_____ Describe any significant experiences in postgraduate school:

_____

_____

What was your major? _____

Give degree and date earned: _____

Describe sports or other extracurricular activities in which you participated, awards you received, and musical instruments you played, throughout your education.

_____

_____

_____

What are your future educational plans?

_____

_____

Vocational History

List the jobs you have held, giving the present or most recent job first. For each job, give the dates you were employed, your job title and salary, and what you liked and disliked about the job.

_____

_____

_____

_____

_____

How often do you miss work at jobs you enjoy? _____

At jobs you dislike? _____

_____

Describe how well you get along with your fellow employees:

_____

_____

Describe how well you get along with your supervisor(s):

_____

_____

What training or education have you had that is relevant to your present occupation?

_____

_____

Does your job satisfy you intellectually? Y/N   emotionally? Y/N   physically? Y/N

What are your vocational ambitions?

_____

_____

What were your childhood interests and hobbies?

_____

_____

What are your present leisure time interests and hobbies?

_____

_____

Religious History

What is the name of your religion?

_____

Describe your most important religious beliefs.

_____

_____

_____

How do your religious beliefs influence the decisions you make in your life?

_____

_____

_____

List your religious activities (prayer, study, meetings, etc.) and how frequently you participate in each one:

_____

_____

_____

Describe how your religious beliefs and those of your parents affected your childhood:

_____

_____

_____

Describe any differences between your religious beliefs and those of your spouse:

_____

_____

_____

Describe any important changes in your religious beliefs during your lifetime:

_____

_____

_____

_____

_____

Opposite Sex Relationship History

List all **significant** opposite-sex relationships you had prior to high school and give the person's name, your age, and the person's age during the relationship, and the duration of the relationship. Indicate if you were in love and if you had a sexual relationship (use separate sheet of paper if needed):

_____

_____

_____

_____

List all **significant** opposite-sex relationships you had during high school and give the person's name, your age, and the person's age during the relationship, and the duration of the relationship. Indicate if you were in love and if you had a sexual relationship (use separate sheet of paper if needed):

_____

_____

_____

_____

_____

List all **significant** opposite-sex relationships you had after high school and give the person's name, your age, and the person's age during the relationship, and the duration of the relationship. Indicate if you were in love and if you had a sexual relationship (use separate sheet of paper if needed):

_____

_____

_____

_____

_____

If you have been divorced, give the name of your former spouse, date married, date divorced, reason for divorce, what you liked most and disliked most about the person, and the names and birth dates of children (use seperate sheet of paper if needed):

_____

_____

_____

_____

_____

If you have been widowed, give the name of your spouse, date married, date and cause of spouse's death, what you liked most and disliked most about your spouse, and the names and birth dates of children (use separate sheet of paper if needed):

_____

_____

_____

_____

_____

Sexual History

When and how did you first learn about sex?

_____

_____

_____

How did your parents influence your attitude regarding sex?

_____

_____

_____

What was your parents' attitude concerning sex? (circle one of the following)
1. Sex was shameful and not to be discussed.
2. Sex was not shameful but it wasn't discussed.
3. Sex was shameful but was also discussed.
4. Sex was not shameful and was freely discussed.

Describe your first sexual experience:

_____

_____

_____

_____

Describe your most important sexual experiences and how they influenced the way you think about sex today:

_____

_____

_____

_____

When and how did you first experience sexual arousal and how did you feel about it?

_____

_____

_____

_____

When and how did you first experience sexual climax and how did you feel about it?

_____

_____

_____

If you have ever masturbated, when did you start? _____

How often did you masturbate during childhood?_____

During adolescence? _____

What sexual fantasies do you have when you masturbate?

_____

_____

_____

When did you first have sexual intercourse and how did the experience affect you?

_____

_____

_____

With how many people have you had sexual intercourse? _____

Have you ever:

    had sexual experiences with or fantasies about being treated violently? Y/N

    had sexual experiences with or fantasies about treating others violently? Y/N

    exposed yourself or desired to expose yourself in public? Y/N

    had sexual contact with children or desired to have sexual contact with children? Y/N

Have you ever been in legal trouble because of your sexual behavior? If so, please describe the behavior and circumstances.

_____

_____

_____

Have you ever had an extramarital sexual relationship(s)? If so, please describe it.

_____

_____

_____

Have you ever had a homosexual experience(s)? If so, please describe it.

_____

_____

_____

Personal Assessment

Describe some of your fears:

_____

_____

_____

Describe faults you think you have:

_____

_____

_____

Describe your good characteristics:

_____

_____

_____

If you ever have any of the thoughts given below, check the frequency of occurrence:

Type of thought	hardly ever	occasionally	frequently
I am lonely.	_____	_____	_____
The future is hopeless.	_____	_____	_____
Nobody cares about me.	_____	_____	_____
I feel like killing myself.	_____	_____	_____
I am a failure.	_____	_____	_____
I am intellectually inferior.	_____	_____	_____
I am going to faint.	_____	_____	_____
I am going to panic.	_____	_____	_____
People don't usually like me.	_____	_____	_____

Other negative thoughts you may have occasionally or frequently:

_____

_____

_____

_____

Indicate the degree that the following problems are a concern to you using this scale:

X = concern in the past, not now

0 = never a concern

1 = very slight degree of concern

2 = mild degree of concern

3 = moderate degree of concern

4 = severe degree of concern

5 = very severe degree of concern

sadness	____	mood swings	____
suicidal feelings	____	verbal or emotional abuse	____
loss of energy	____	physical abuse	____
low self-esteem	____	sexual abuse	____
isolation and loneliness	____	financial problems	____
sleep disturbance	____	career problems	____
headaches	____	marital problems	____
dizziness	____	parent/child problems	____
angry feelings	____		

Goals for Personal Improvement

Below is a list of bad habits and uncomfortable feelings that may include some that are making you feel anxious and depressed. Check off any habits or uncomfortable feelings that you would like to change:

____ drinking alcoholic beverages too much

____ smoking too much

____ using drugs too much—name the drug(s) _____

____ eating too much

____ exercising too little

____ feeling too much attraction to members of my own sex

____ feeling too much attraction to members of the opposite sex

____ feeling nauseated when nervous

239

____ thinking depressing thoughts

____ feeling anxious in crowds

____ feeling anxious in high places

____ worrying about my health

____ feeling anxious in airplanes

____ stuttering

____ washing my hands too often

____ cleaning and straightening things up too often

____ biting my fingernails

____ being careless of my physical appearance

____ feeling anxious in enclosed places

____ feeling anxious in open places

____ being too afraid of blood

____ feeling anxious about contamination or germs

____ feeling anxious about being alone

____ feeling afraid of darkness

____ feeling afraid of certain animals

____ thinking the same thoughts over and over

____ counting my heartbeats

____ hearing voices

____ feeling people are against me or out to get me

____ seeing visions or objects that aren't really there

____ wetting the bed at night or having difficulty controlling my bladder

____ having difficulty controlling my bowel movement

____ taking too much medicine

____ having too many headaches

____ gambling too much

____ being unable to fall asleep at night

____ exposing my body to strangers

____ wearing clothes of the opposite sex

____ feeling sexually attracted to other people's clothing or belongings

____ feeling sexually attracted to children

____ feeling sexually attracted to animals

____ feeling a sexual desire to hurt other people

____ feeling a sexual desire to be hurt or humiliated

____ feeling a nonsexual desire to hurt other people

____ feeling a nonsexual desire to be hurt or humiliated

____ stealing or a desire to steal

____ lying

____ yelling at people when I'm angry

____ poor management of money

____ saying foolish things to people

____ having difficulty carrying on a conversation with people

____ bothering or irritating people too much

____ forgetfulness

____ contemplating suicide

____ setting fires or a desire to set fires

____ difficulty being steadily employed

____ feeling uncomfortable at work

____ swearing

____ being too upset when criticized by others

____ having difficulty expressing feelings

____ putting things off that need to be done

____ thinking things that cause guilty feelings

____ feeling anxious when work is being supervised

____ feeling anxious about sexual thoughts

____ feeling anxious about kissing

____ feeling anxious about petting

____ feeling anxious about sexual intercourse

____ having difficulty making decisions when they need to be made

____ feeling uncomfortable with groups of people

____ feeling anxious about: _____

_____

_____

_____

____ feeling depressed about: _____

_____

_____

_____

____ feeling guilty about: _____

_____

_____

_____

____ being unable to control my desire to: _____

_____

_____

_____

How do you plan to change the habits and/or uncomfortable feelings checked above?

_____

_____

_____

_____

_____

L O V E B U S T E R S
QUESTIONNAIRE

This questionnaire is designed to help identify your spouse's Love Busters. Your spouse engages in a Love Buster whenever one of his or her habits causes you to be unhappy. By causing your unhappiness, he or she withdraws love units from the account in your Love Bank, and that, in turn, threatens your romantic love for him or her.

There are five categories of Love Busters. Each category has its own set of questions in this questionnaire. Answer all the questions as candidly as possible. Do not try to minimize your unhappiness with your spouse's behavior. If your answers require more space, use and attach a separate sheet of paper.

When you have completed this questionnaire, go through it a second time to be certain your answers accurately reflect your feelings. Do not erase your original answers, but cross them out lightly so that your spouse can see the corrections and discuss them with you.

The final page of this questionnaire asks you to rank the five Love Busters in order of their importance to you. When you have finished ranking the Love Busters, you may find that your answers to the questions regarding each Love Buster are inconsistent with your final ranking. This inconsistency is common. It often reflects a less than perfect understanding of your feelings. If you notice inconsistencies, discuss them with your spouse to help clarify your feelings.

You have the permission of the publisher to photocopy the questionnaire for use in your own marriage. I recommend that you enlarge it 125 percent so that you'll have plenty of room to write in your responses. Make two copies, one for you and one for your spouse.

1. **Angry Outbursts.** Deliberate attempts by your spouse to hurt you because of anger toward you. They are usually in the form of verbal or physical attacks.

   A. **Angry Outbursts as a Cause of Unhappiness:** Indicate how much unhappiness you tend to experience when your spouse attacks you with an angry outburst.

0	1	2	3	4	5	6

   I experience   I experience   I experience
   no unhappiness   moderate unhappiness   extreme unhappiness

   B. **Frequency of Spouse's Angry Outbursts:** Indicate how often your spouse tends to engage in angry outbursts toward you.

   _____(write number) angry outbursts each day/week/month/ year (circle one).

   C. **Form(s) Angry Outbursts Take:** When your spouse engages in angry outbursts toward you, what does he or she typically do?_____
   _____
   _____

   D. **Form of Angry Outbursts That Causes the Greatest Unhappiness:** Which of the above forms of angry outbursts causes you the greatest unhappiness?_____
   _____
   _____

   E. **Onset of Angry Outbursts:** When did your spouse first engage in angry outbursts toward you?_____
   _____
   _____
   _____

   F. **Development of Angry Outbursts:** Have your spouse's angry outbursts increased or decreased in intensity and/or frequency since they first began? How do recent angry outbursts compare to those of the past?_____
   _____
   _____
   _____

2. **Disrespectful Judgments.** Attempts by your spouse to change your attitudes, beliefs, and behavior by trying to force you into his way of thinking. If (1) your spouse lectures you instead of respectfully discussing issues, (2) feels that his or her opinion is superior to yours, (3) talks over you or prevents you from having a chance to explain your position, or (4) ridicules your point of view, your spouse is engaging in disrespectful judgments.

   A. **Disrespectful Judgments as a Cause of Unhappiness:** Indicate how much unhappiness you tend to experience when your spouse engages in disrespectful judgments toward you.

   | 0 | 1 | 2 | 3 | 4 | 5 | 6 |

   I experience   I experience   I experience
   no unhappiness   moderate unhappiness   extreme unhappiness

   B. **Frequency of Spouse's Disrespectful Judgments:** Indicate how often your spouse tends to engage in disrespectful judgments toward you.

   _____ (write number) disrespectful judgments each day/week/month/ year (circle one).

   C. **Form(s) Disrespectful Judgments Take:** When your spouse engages in disrespectful judgments toward you, what does he or she typically do? _____

   _____

   D. **Form of Disrespectful Judgments That Causes the Greatest Unhappiness:** Which of the above forms of disrespectful judgments causes you the greatest unhappiness?_____

   _____

   _____

   E. **Onset of Disrespectful Judgments:** When did your spouse first engage in disrespectful judgments toward you?_____

   _____

   _____

   F. **Development of Disrespectful Judgments:** Have your spouse's disrespectful judgments increased or decreased in intensity and/or frequency since they first began? How do recent disrespectful judgments compare to those of the past?_____

   _____

   _____

3. **Annoying Behavior.** The two basic types of annoying behavior are habits and activities. Habits are repeated without much thought, such as the way your spouse eats or sits in a chair. Activities are usually scheduled and require thought to complete, such as attending sporting events or engaging in a personal exercise program. Habits and activities are "annoying behavior" if they cause you to feel unhappy. They can be as innocent as snoring or as destructive as infidelity or alcohol addiction.

A. **Annoying Behavior as a Cause of Unhappiness:** Indicate how much unhappiness you tend to experience when your spouse engages in annoying behavior.

0	1	2	3	4	5	6

I experience no unhappiness   I experience moderate unhappiness   I experience extreme unhappiness

B. **Frequency of Spouse's Annoying Behavior:** Indicate how often your spouse tends to engage in annoying behavior.

_____ (write number) occurrences of annoying behavior each day/week/month/year (circle one).

C. **Form(s) Annoying Behavior Takes:** When your spouse engages in annoying behavior toward you, what does he or she typically do?_____
_____
_____

D. **Form of Annoying Behavior That Causes the Greatest Unhappiness:** Which of the above forms of annoying behavior causes you the greatest unhappiness?_____
_____
_____

E. **Onset of Annoying Behavior:** When did your spouse first engage in annoying behavior?_____
_____
_____

F. **Development of Annoying Behavior:** Has your spouse's annoying behavior increased or decreased in intensity and/or frequency since it first began? How does recent annoying behavior compare to that of the past?_____
_____
_____

4. Selfish Demands. Attempts by your spouse to force you to do something for him or her, usually with implied threat of punishment if you refuse.

A. Selfish Demands as a Cause of Unhappiness: Indicate how much unhappiness you tend to experience when your spouse makes selfish demands of you.

```
0        1        2        3        4        5        6
|--------|--------|--------|--------|--------|--------|
I experience          I experience          I experience
no unhappiness        moderate unhappiness  extreme unhappiness
```

B. Frequency of Spouse's Selfish Demands: Indicate how often your spouse makes selfish demands of you.

_____ (write number) selfish demands each day/week/month/year (circle one).

C. Form(s) Selfish Demands Take: When your spouse makes selfish demands of you, what does he or she typically do?_____

_____

_____

_____

D. Form of Selfish Demands That Causes the Greatest Unhappiness: Which of the above forms of selfish demands causes you the greatest unhappiness?_____

_____

_____

_____

E. Onset of Selfish Demands: When did your spouse first make selfish demands of you?_____

_____

_____

_____

F. Development of Selfish Demands: Have your spouse's selfish demands increased or decreased in intensity and/or frequency since they first began? How do recent selfish demands compare to those of the past?

_____

_____

_____

5. **Dishonesty.** Failure of your spouse to reveal his or her thoughts, feelings, habits, likes, dislikes, personal history, daily activities, and plans for the future. Dishonesty is not only providing false information about any of the above topics, but it is also leaving you with what your spouse knows is a false impression.

    A. Dishonesty as a Cause of Unhappiness: Indicate how much unhappiness you tend to experience when your spouse is dishonest with you.

```
0        1        2        3        4        5        6
|_____|_____|_____|_____|_____|_____|
I experience          I experience          I experience
no unhappiness     moderate unhappiness   extreme unhappiness
```

    B. Frequency of Spouse's Dishonesty: Indicate how often your spouse tends to be dishonest with you.

    _____ (write number) instances of dishonesty each day/week/month/year (circle one).

    C. Form(s) Dishonesty Takes: When your spouse is dishonest with you, what does he or she typically do? _____
_____
_____

    D. Form of Dishonesty That Causes the Greatest Unhappiness: Which of the above forms of dishonesty causes you the greatest unhappiness?
_____
_____
_____

    E. Onset of Dishonesty: When was your spouse first dishonest with you?
_____
_____
_____

    F. Development of Dishonesty: Has your spouse's dishonesty increased or decreased in intensity and/or frequency since it first began? How do recent instances of dishonesty compare to those of the past? _____
_____
_____
_____

Rating Love Busters

The five basic categories of Love Busters are listed below. There is also space for you to add other categories of Love Busters that you feel contribute to your marital unhappiness. In the space provided in front of each Love Buster, write a number from 1 to 5 that ranks its relative contribution to your unhappiness. Write a 1 before the Love Buster that causes you the greatest unhappiness, a 2 before the one causing the next greatest unhappiness, and so on, until you have ranked all five.

_____ Angry Outbursts
_____ Disrespectful Judgments
_____ Annoying Behavior
_____ Selfish Demands
_____ Dishonesty

_____ _____
_____ _____

Agreement to Overcome Love Busters

This Agreement is made this _____ day of _____
between _____ and _____ ,
whereby it is mutually agreed:

_____ will learn to avoid the following Love
Busters:

1. _____
2. _____
3. _____
4. _____
5. _____

_____ will learn to avoid the following Love
Busters:

1. _____
2. _____
3. _____
4. _____
5. _____

In Witness Whereof, the parties hereto have signed this agreement on the day
and year first above written:

_____   _____
His signature   Her signature

ABOUT THE AUTHOR

Willard F. Harley, Jr., Ph.D., is a clinical psychologist and marriage counselor. Over the past twenty-five years he has helped thousands of couples overcome marital conflict and restore their love for each other. His innovative counseling methods are described in the books and articles he writes. Dr. Harley also leads training workshops for couples and marriage counselors and has appeared on hundreds of radio and television programs.

Willard Harley and Joyce, his wife of more than thirty years, live in White Bear Lake, Minnesota. They are parents of two married children who are also marriage counselors.

Be sure to visit Dr. Harley's web site at:
http://www.marriagebuilders.com.

New in 2002!

In store: January 2002
Hardcover

I Cherish You

Give others the knowledge to build a lifelong, romantic love! *I Cherish You* highlights the concepts of *His Needs, Her Needs* in a beautiful gift format—perfect for celebrating a wedding or anniversary, or just to say "I love you."

What does it take to make your marriage *sizzle?*

FIFTEENTH ANNIVERSARY EDITION

HIS NEEDS HER NEEDS

Building an Affair-Proof Marriage

Willard F. Harley, Jr.

MORE THAN 1,000,000 COPIES SOLD

Hardcover
224 pages

In this classic book, Willard Harley identifies the ten most vital needs of men and women and shows husbands and wives how to satisfy those needs in their spouses. He provides guidance for becoming irresistible to your spouse and for loving more creatively and sensitively, thereby eliminating the problems that often lead to extramarital affairs.

Love Busters
Overcoming Habits That Destroy Romantic Love
Hardcover, 192 pages

A guide to identifying and overcoming five common but dangerous habits that destroy romantic love.

Five Steps to Romantic Love
A Workbook for Readers of Love Busters *and* His Needs, Her Needs
Paperback, 192 pages

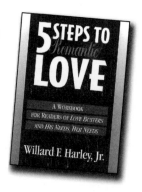

A helpful workbook containing all the contracts, questionnaires, inventories, and worksheets Dr. Harley recommends in *Love Busters* and *His Needs, Her Needs*.

Surviving an Affair
Hardcover, 224 pages

A guide to understanding and surviving every aspect of infidelity—from the beginning of an affair through the restoration of the marriage.

VISIT DR. HARLEY'S WEB SITE—

http://www.marriagebuilders.com

"Building Marriages to Last a Lifetime"

Dr. Harley has saved thousands of marriages from the pain of unresolved conflict and the disaster of divorce. His successful approach to building marriages can help you too.

Why do people fall in love? Why do they fall out of love? What do they want most in marriage? What drives them out of marriage? How can a bad marriage become a great marriage? Dr. Harley's basic concepts address these and other important aspects of marriage building.

At the Marriage Builders web site Dr. Harley introduces visitors to some of the best ways to overcome marital conflicts and some of the quickest ways to restore love. From the pages of "Basic Concepts" and articles by Dr. Harley to the archives for his weekly Q&A columns and information about upcoming seminars, this site is packed with useful material.

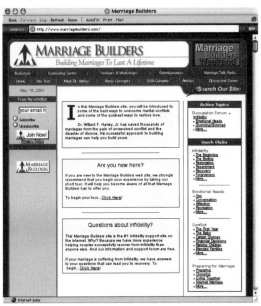

Let Marriage Builders help you build a marriage to last a lifetime!